THIS FOUL THING CALLED WAR

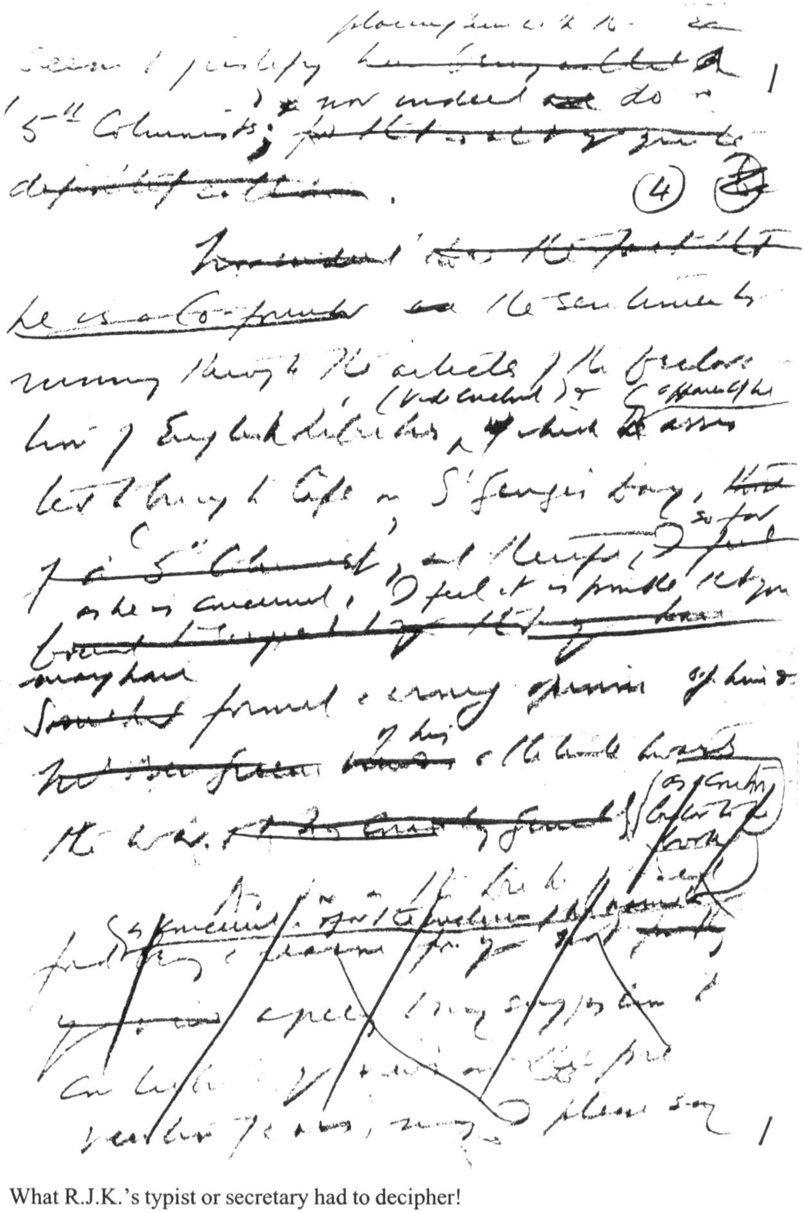

What R.J.K.'s typist or secretary had to decipher!

THIS FOUL THING CALLED WAR

*The Life Of Brigadier-General R.J. Kentish,
CMG, DSO (1876–1956)*

Basil Kentish

The Book Guild Ltd
Sussex, England

The Book Guild Ltd.
25 High Street,
Lewes, Sussex

First published 1997
© Basil Kentish, 1997

Set in Times
Typesetting by
Raven Typesetters, Chester

Printed in Great Britain by
Bookcraft (Bath) Ltd, Avon

A catalogue record for this book is
available from the British Library

ISBN 1 85776 295 9

CONTENTS

PREFACE

Brigadier General R.J. Kentish, CMG, DSO

Field Marshal Sir Gerald Templer, Chief of the Imperial General Staff and Colonel of my uncle's old Regiment, the Royal Irish Fusiliers, said of him on a public occasion at Aldershot in 1957:

> Brigadier Reggie Kentish was one of the most forceful personalities the Army has produced in the last few generations.... He should be remembered for devoting a large part of his life to the improvement of the conditions under which soldiers lived — improvements brought about despite constant opposition from the old-fashioned.

The Duke of Sutherland, in *The Times* obituary column, had written in 1956:

> I remembered so well working with General Kentish when I was President of the British Olympic Association and again when organising the National Playing Fields Association. His wonderful enthusiasm and unbounded energy helped tremendously to steer us through numerous difficulties ... I am delighted to add my tribute to the efforts of a great worker and a most kindly gentleman.

My uncle's own obituary notice in *The Times* in 1956 said, inter-alia:

> He frequently represented the United Kingdom at meetings of the International Olympic Committee and there his advice was much sought after by representatives of other nations. It was always

willingly given, usually followed, and nearly always proved to be right.

An unidentified writer, T.E.L., added this to the obituary column:

> As a temporary officer I attended General Kentish's Third Army School at Flixécourt in 1916. Later I attended his Senior Officers School at Aldershot and I have always remembered him. He was an inspired teacher and leader of men. No one who attended his lectures could fail to catch something of his enthusiasm for the Army or feel with him his trust and pride in the British soldier.
>
> To us young officers a General was a fearsome thing, but although his discipline was strict he was always kind and considerate, and he was never pompous ... He taught us the meaning of morale and how to delegate and trust our subordinates and many other things which we who had the honour of knowing him shall not forget.

These are the things people remembered about him after his death. The key word throughout is enthusiastic — but to this should be added the words unorthodox and eccentric.

My uncle, born in 1876, was known to his friends, acquaintances and contemporaries as 'Reggie Kentish' or 'R.J.K.', but he liked to be called 'General' by those younger or junior to him, despite the fact that the rank had been abolished after 1918 in favour of Brigadier. Domesticity was not a strong point, nor was there ever any inclination on his part to alter his mode of living, even if it could be achieved. Consequently he remained unmarried until his death in 1956, for no sane woman was willing to take on such a formidable proposition. Thus, after leaving the Army in 1922, he drifted from one hotel in London to the other: Baileys in Gloucester Road, The Rembrandt in Brompton Road, The Hyde Park in Knightsbridge, The Piccadilly, The Grosvenor near Victoria Station and, finally, The Dorchester in Park Lane. After the outbreak of the Second World War he evacuated himself to less prodigious hostelries in the South of England, staying each time until the management said, 'Enough, General'.

Insisting on the observance of points of etiquette and the conventions of everyday life by others, he regarded himself as an exception to the rule. How many people in this world have shaken the Pope by the hand instead of kissing his ring? He cared not a bit for those in authority over him. As much at home with the Establishment as with the man in the street, he manipulated the former for the benefit of the less articulate members of society. He never owned or drove a car, nor did he ever vote in an election; if he had stood for Parliament, he would have called himself a Labour-Imperialist. Impetuous and heedless of higher authority, he was difficult to live with.

He had a burning enthusiasm for anything he undertook, which infected those who worked with him. His greatest asset was his ability to talk – and talk he certainly did – and be on perfectly good terms with all classes for society, from Kings and Dictators down to those he regarded as the least privileged to whose welfare he devoted the greater part of his life. His ideals and aims were clear cut from an early age. As the last century was nearing its end, so he realised that there was a great gap between the undernourished youth in a dockland slum and the Public Schoolboy with acres of playing fields at his disposal; between the soldier of the time, who drank great quantities of beer through sheer boredom, and his officers on the polo ground. Hence his crusade for the building of sports grounds in the Army before 1914 and his foundation of the National Playing Fields Association in 1924, '*mens sana in corpore sano*' being his motto.

Perhaps one can conjure up the vision of a religious man with a celestial halo – but he was nothing of the kind. An extrovert, a lover of all forms of sports and pastimes, a bon viveur, a raconteur, an inveterate leg-puller, he enjoyed life to the full, and a bit over.

He was clearly no slouch with the pen. He wrote and wrote incessantly – when he was not talking – or, more correctly, he scribbled and scribbled, often through the night, with a hiero-glyphic scrawl which only his close relatives or a gifted secretary or typist could decipher. Amongst many items of a literary nature which he left behind him was an unpublished typescript called '100 Incidents In My Life', written at the instigation of Ward Price of the *Daily Mail* during the Second World War. This contained amusing stories of encounters which he had had with people, ranging from most of the crowned, or ex-crowned, heads of

Europe down to the cockney urchin who said to his mate, ' 'Arry, there's a toff! Wonder what he wears on Sunday?'. 'The suit I've got on! It's the only one I have in the world, and I sleep in it too, spats and all,' rejoined my uncle quickly. 'Well, wevver yer sleeps in it or wevver yer dussn't, you're a regular toff,' said the lad.

He also left behind him, typed but not published, a potential book he had written in 1943, when the Second World War was going through a dreary and not too hopeful stage. He had sent a questionnaire to 80 people of distinction asking them who, in their opinion, was responsible in England for letting us in for the War – and unprepared at that. Should the guilty men be impeached and brought to trial? And, finally, what steps should be taken to prevent the outbreak of the Third World War? About 30 of the 80 replied at length, including Sir Winston Churchill, H.G. Wells and the Master of Trinity College, Cambridge.

I hope the memories of this unorthodox man – and my own memories of him too – will give a picture of certain aspects of life during the last 75 years of the British Empire. My uncle should be remembered for his enthusiasm and lack of fear of higher authority which enabled him to push aside opposition from the old fashioned in order, as the Rev. Howard Marshall said at his memorial service in 1956, 'to make a flickering candle burn more brightly for the welfare of the nation'.

The ensuing narrative begins out of sequence, with a chapter on the Battle of the Somme in France in 1916, because the year 1996 marks the 80th anniversary of this horrendous and now legendary event.

1

'The Keening of a Thousand Banshees'

The year 1996 marks the 80th anniversary of the Battle of the Somme, which commenced on 1 July 1916 at 7.30 a.m. By the end of the first day there had been nearly 60,000 British casualties. The battle continued into November, by which time we had only penetrated six miles into the German defences at a cost of nearly half a million dead, wounded or missing. After 80 years there can be very few survivors to recall memories of the battle, even though many men had enlisted at the age of 15 or 16, but it still evokes the interest of present generations, both in the written word and guided tours to the battlefield or the many war cemeteries.

In the early days of 1916 the French and British governments decided on a Big Push, as it was called, to try to end the static warfare conditions of 1915. Unfortunately the plans came to naught: the Germans attacked the French at Verdun with such ferocity that it became doubtful whether the defenders could hold on for much longer. A diversion was necessary; the British had not only to make it but to carry out the Big Push on their own. This was a political decision and the C-in-C, British Expeditionary Force, General Douglas Haig, was not optimistic, although he was convinced that the war against Germany would be won in France and nowhere else. In the end he was correct.

It fell to the lot of General Henry Rawlinson's 4th Army to initiate the attack. He had the 1st, 2nd and 3rd Armies to the north of him, and his southern boundary was the River Somme and the left flank of the French line. His plan was to attack with 15 Infantry Divisions on a 15-mile front in an easterly direction in order to

1

make the initial breakthrough, after which three Cavalry Divisions, held in GHQ reserve, would advance through the gap to exploit the success. His only real worry was the fact that nine of these Divisions were mainly composed of Kitchener's New Army, half trained and untried in battle – yet all enthusiastic volunteers who were 'rarin' to go'.

The 4th Army plan was simple (on paper); an Artillery bombardment would pound the German positions for five days and five nights to destroy them together with their occupants. The 15 Divisions would then advance in extended order at a slow pace to occupy the, hopefully, unmanned German trenches. At 7.30 a.m. on 1 July, therefore, after the artillery bombardment had stopped, thousand upon thousand of men went over the top, only to discover that it was no walkover; they had walked into a living hell. The Germans had built a system of very deep dugouts in which the men had sheltered during the prolonged barrage. Now they emerged to man their machine guns, which mowed the attackers down at the start of their hoped-for leisurely stroll to victory. To make matters worse, our guns had used a large proportion of shrapnel shells, the bullets from which had no effect on the enemy barbed wire, much of which was still intact. Many of those who reached it died on it. After months of detailed planning, orders, instructions, advice and rehearsals, 57,000 casualties had been incurred with very little to show for this, the most tragic day for Britain in the War.

As the gunfire during that evening was dying down, a party of the 6th Battalion, the West Yorkshire Regiment, was sent up the line as reinforcements. The progress of these bewildered men is poignantly described by Lyn MacDonald in his book *The Somme*, published in 1983 by Michael Joseph.

> As they neared the wood, between the roar of explosions, behind the sickening gas-soaked mist, in the forefront of the noise that raged at them from every horizon, the small party of the West Yorkshires became aware of another sound. It was like nothing they had ever heard before. Later – and for the rest of his life – Lt. Hornshaw was to remember it as a sound that chilled the blood; a nerve-scraping noise like 'enormous wet fingers screeching across an enormous pane of glass'. It was coming from the wounded,

lying out in No Man's Land. Some screaming, some muttering, some weeping with fear, some calling for help, shouting in delirium, groaning with pain, the sounds of their distress had synthesised into one unearthly wail. As midnight passed and the night of the first day of July turned towards the dawn of the second, as the gunfire died down, it seemed to fill the air. All along the front, from the orchards of Gommecourt to the heights of Beaumont Hamel, from the shoulders of Thiepval to the valley beyond La Boiselle, it rose from the battlefield into the night like the keening of a thousand banshees.

Where does my uncle come into all this? The Battle of the Somme lasted all that summer and into November, by which time the ground was a treacherous sea of mud and the weather decidedly inclement. Offensive operations were regularly carried out on a localized scale, with varying degrees of success but with heavy casualties. R.J.K. was commanding 76 Infantry Brigade in the 3rd Division. Personnel at a Brigade HQ formed the middle layer of a sandwich. They were not called upon to rise from the trenches with fixed bayonets to try to make contact with the enemy, yet they were sporadically subjected to the crump of German shells, which might often cause deadly havoc. On the other hand, they were remote from the rear echelons, Divisional, Corps and Army HQs, which traditionally lived in comfortable chateaux and whose denizens were reputedly ignorant of the living conditions endured by the fighting soldier. Furthest away, of course, was General Haig's HQ at Montreuil, some 25 miles from the front line.

During the period 14–26 July a minor offensive by several Divisions was carried out in an area which included Delville Wood and the village of Longueval. As part of the 3rd Division, my uncle's 76th Infantry Brigade was involved. Afterwards, on 3 August, he sent a report on 116 pages of foolscap to the Divisional Commander, Major-General Cyril Deverill, criticizing the way in which operational orders were issued by higher commanders and the tactics included in them. In addition, there was criticism of matters relating to organization, administration and staff duties. With due humility, R.J.K. suggested how these defects could be rectified if future operations were to be more successful, with fewer casualties.

3

There was a consensus of opinion, he thought, amongst Brigadiers and line officers that there had been too much rush. Those directing operations from behind should time their orders to give local commanders the opportunity to make the necessary reconnaissance of the ground with the men who were to carry out the assault. He quoted examples of where this had been possible – with complete success as a result – and where it had not been possible – with a failed attack and much loss of life. Then he recommended that tired troops after an attack should not be asked to consolidate the new positions; they were an easy prey to a sudden counter-attack by the enemy. Tired troops should be immediately relieved, although a few units who knew the situation should be kept *in situ* temporarily during the relief.

He deplored the passing back of information that a position had been secured or, alternatively, that the troops involved had been cut up with no survivors, without the confirmation first of a responsible person; wildcat or untrue reports could vitally affect a subsequent attack. Furthermore, he deplored the reinforcement of infantry units with men from other Regiments; it was disastrous for morale. He would rather, as an Infantry Commander, go into battle with 300 men belonging to the Regiment than 700 men, 400 of whom had been hurriedly gathered in from four or five different units. Finally he asked that any Division which had gone through intense fighting with heavy casualties should have at least 28 days in which to recuperate, and not be put back again into the same sector.

Fearing that this long report would go no further than 3rd Division HQ, he skipped an echelon, i.e. Corps, and sent a copy to Major-General Archibald Montgomery, Chief of Staff to General Rawlinson, commanding the 4th Army. In doing so he was treading on dangerous ground, for, in 1901, when a subaltern in South Africa during the Boer War, he had had an encounter with Rawlinson. 'You are an impertinent young officer,' he had said, 'what is your name?' Writing the name Kentish on a piece of paper, he continued, 'If you should come before me for promotion in later years,I shall do this,' and, tearing up the scrap of paper, he threw it in the waste-paper basket. Rawlinson had come in for criticism over his abortive effort on 1 July; apart from anything else, he had disregarded advice from Haig on two points which, it followed, might have turned a disaster into a victory. Haig had recommended that (i) the artillery bombardment should only last for three days, and (ii) that the attacking troops should advance at a quick pace behind a creeping barrage, which would keep the heads of the German down until the very last moment. But, being a cavalry man, he had deferred to Rawlinson, an infantry soldier. But R.J.K. was never afraid, all his life, to attack higher authority if it would benefit the 'underdog'.

A month later, R.J.K. was sent back to England, to organize and to be first Commandant of the new Senior Officers School in Aldershot, through which every officer had to pass before being allowed to command his battalion in action. This indeed was an appointment carrying great responsibility. It could hardly be said that he had been 'degummed', but, as will be seen later, it is very probable that GHQ in France was glad to see the last of this infernal nuisance, who was looked upon in the rear areas as an Antichrist.

And so the Battle of the Somme dragged on into the autumn, which is when my father makes a brief appearance into the story. He was, at this time, Brigade Major, 14th Infantry Brigade, and, like his brother, in the middle of the sandwich, so to speak. He had retired from the Royal Fusiliers in 1906, but had been recalled to the Active List in 1914 after eight years as a civilian, hence the great discrepancy in rank between himself and his brother, R.J.K.

In November a small offensive was launched, demanded by the politicians, near the River Ancre, a tributary of the Somme. After the War a Brigade Commander during the battle wrote:

> The Army Commander and his staff simply had no conception of the condition of the forward area, which was, in fact, the worst I can remember at any time in the war. The ground was one huge morass of slimy mud.... The men in the line lived in mud and water over their knees ... I fear HQ, 5th Army, was blissfully unconscious, living as they did in a substantial chateau several miles behind the line.

Also after the war, on 19 November 1936, my father wrote to Brig.

Gen. Sir James Edmonds, who was writing the Official War History, France 1916:

> I shall never forget the details of that day. It was bitterly cold with a blinding snow storm which from time to time turned to hail and rain. The Staff Officer from GHQ who is reported to have wept at the sight of the mud at Passchendaele would still be mopping his eyes if he had been with me that morning. This was the only occasion when I saw men dead from exhaustion from their efforts to get out of the mud. At Passchendaele I saw men mudbound but they could be dragged out, but in the Ancre at this time we were pitchforked into the quagmire in the dark and there was no possibility of a man helping the one next to him.... As I have said before, many of the casualties were untouched by shell or bullet.
>
> It was the very worst instance I came across of what appeared to be a cruel useless sacrifice of life, and the climatic conditions alone made it clear from the start to the very stupidest brain that no success could possibly result. Two days after the so-called attack the Divisional Commander, his two General Staff Officers, two Brigadiers and two Brigade Majors were removed. My Brigadier several times said to me, 'Kentish, I can not send your reports in, I should lose my job!' But he did lose it after all.
>
> The question I have never had answered is this: Is an officer justified in cancelling on his own initiative an attack which he knows no sane General would ever sanction if he himself were on the spot?

Thus, at the end of November, the Battle of the Somme came to an end, at a cost of 400,000 casualties and a total advance of six miles at the outside. The breakthrough had not been achieved, but pressure had been taken off the French at Verdun; they were still in the War. The troops settled down to the rigours of the winter; the three Cavalry Divisions, after pawing the ground for four months, retired from the scene unused.

'Are we to continue until we have killed ALL our young men?' asked Lord Landsdowne in a memorandum to the Cabinet. Apparently so, for the Cabinet was happy to postpone further aggressive action until spring of 1917. Final victory was not to come until November 1918, so justifying Haig's conviction that the War would be decided on the Western Front.

2

A Social Conscience

Reggie Kentish, or R.J.K., second son of George and Caroline Kentish, was born in 1876. He was not of a traditional Army family. In 1870 his father had come into possession of the publishing business of W.H. Hayden, 13 Paternoster Row, London EC1, and also the freehold of a seventeenth-century house nearby in Warwick Square, where the family lived. From the windows at the back could be seen the spot where the gallows had formerly been erected, near Newgate Jail, when a public hanging was to take place.

Shortly after his birth the family moved to Bexley, about a dozen miles from the Metropolis. My uncle's earliest remembrance was being taken, at the age of eight, by the family nanny to have his golden curls removed. When they emerged from the barber's shop a man was selling papers and calling out, 'Fall of Khartoum – death of General Gordon'. Another memory from Bexley, one which had an effect on his later life, was the strictness of the Victorian Sabbath. 'It was,' he wrote long after, 'a real nightmare. We all had to be dressed in our best clothes and spend the greater part of the day being marched to and from interminable services, not understanding one single word that was spoken or gabbled by the Vicar or his Curate. The service frequently lasted nearly two hours with a sermon well over half an hour. Then came Sunday School, followed by a long evening service. Nothing in my after life set me against the Church so much as those early days of my youth.'

Doubtless it was these early memories which must have turned

7

him against the compulsory Sunday church parade in the Army. In 1908 at Aldershot he was to have a heart-to-heart talk with a young padre who had complained to a higher authority that the men coughed and shuffled their feet during services. R.J.K. said:

> It would be bad enough if your congregation had come voluntarily. The forcing of the soldier to go to church is breaking God's Fourth Commandment: Remember the Sabbath Day and keep it holy ... on the seventh day thou shalt do no work. Yet the soldier has to get ready for parade the night before, getting his ceremonial kit spick and span. On the next day he is inspected with the prospect of being punished if his equipment is dirty; then he is marched to church and back again afterwards. The sooner this obnoxious and un-English parade, benefiting neither God, chaplain, soldier or church, becomes a thing of the past, the better for all concerned. But this is a question for Higher Authority; we are here to talk about coughing and the making of other noises.
>
> So cut your sermon by half. Don't talk over their heads – they are only young lads – threatening them with hell-fire, but talk about something which will interest them. They are all, for instance, keen on sport; subjects such as the Team Spirit or we must all pull together will make them listen to you without coughing or shuffling their feet. But, first of all, go to see them playing their games, have a drink with them in the canteen; be human.

At the end of this homily Padre Little expressed gratification and promised to alter his ways at once.

The house in Bexley soon became too small; the household, including staff, now numbered 13, so a move was made to Oaklands Park in Bromley, followed, in 1900, by a move to a house in South Kensington. This was a typical terraced house of six storeys – nowadays all converted into flats – in which the domestic staff crept down from the attic floor to the basement at the crack of dawn, to light the kitchen range or prepare the early morning tea and hot water (in brass cans) for the family three or four floors higher. This was only the beginning of a long day in which the cook, perhaps, was the luckiest.

In Bexley R.J.K. and his three brothers went to a small day school kept by a benevolent old man called Rowsell. Then his

8

father discovered that a gentleman of the name Kentish had left a considerable sum of money, the interest from which was to be devoted to the free education at St. Albans Grammar School of any boy bearing his name. So the four brothers, each in turn, were despatched to the School, where the headmaster lodged and fed about a dozen boys in his own house.

From there, in 1892, he went to Malvern College in Worcestershire with a classical scholarship of £50 a year in his pocket, to be followed in due course by his two younger brothers. Here he achieved a considerable reputation as an athlete, as well as being Captain of the Football XI, Captain of the Cross-Country Running team and winner of the half-mile swimming race in the River Severn. Additionally, he was a School Prefect and a Lieutenant in the Officers Training Corps.

The outcome of his public school education, i.e. the effect on his later life, is described by him much later, probably after the Second World War.

Today the whole question of education generally, and of our Public Schools in particular, is probably as much discussed as any of our post-war problems. It may be out of place if I make reference to our Public School system and all that it meant to England and to the building up of our Empire in the past. Let me say that I have worn an 'old school tie' ever since I left Malvern. But this does not mean that I regard the system as the most perfect one for educating our boys and girls. On the contrary, in certain respects, it is about the worst possible system and it will have to undergo very radical alterations.

When a boy leaves a Public School and goes into the world to mix with his fellow men, the fact stands out that during his school days no word is said to him regarding his attitude towards other classes of people with whom he is bound to come into contact. The direct result of this is that he grows up into manhood thinking that, chiefly because he has been sent to an expensive school barred to others, he is a very much superior kind of person – a member of the 'Old School Tie Brigade'.

Not a single word is said to him by his masters regarding his good fortune in being born to parents well enough off to send him to a Public School or of the misfortune of thousands of others who have not had his good fortune. Not a word does he hear from his masters of the miserable conditions of life of the masses or what he can do to alleviate their lot if and when he meets them, as meet them he must, when he goes out into the world.

Not a word of this ever came to my ears the whole of the time I spent at Malvern; four happy years with good food and splendid cricket and football pitches. I was never told how fortunate I was to have plenty of good food when there were probably masses of poorer boys who, if not near the border line of starvation, went to bed at the end of the day feeling hungry. Or how fortunate I was to be able to play games when these other thousands of boys were longing to do so, but unable to simply because there were no public playing fields for them to play on. Not a word of this ever came to my ears the whole time I was at Malvern until the end of my last term when I took the school football team to Canning Town, E17, to play a friendly match against a team of Dockland boys. This had been arranged by the Reverend G.P. Gillett who was in charge of the Malvern Mission in that part of London. It was the first time a team from Malvern had done this; possibly the first match ever played by a Public School against boys from the so-called working classes. After the match was over we were taken round by the Missioner to see the Mission buildings and then the homes of the boys who had been our opponents on the football pitch on the Beckton Marshes, and the conditions under which they existed. I will not say lived, for the conditions were just indescribable. It was quite possible that I might have remained in blissful ignorance, were it not for this occasion, of the meaning of 'slum life' and of the great divide which existed then – and still does to a lesser degree today – between the various social classes.

Fortunately I saw the picture myself, and I never forgot it to this day. I have, in fact, never allowed it out of my sight and I can say with all sincerity that, no matter what my job or occupation has been, I have never ceased by word and deed to help those who, by accident of birth, have been born into the world and brought up in far less favourable circumstances than I was. The older I got and the higher the position I attained, the greater I found were the powers and the opportunities I had of helping and adding to their happiness or comfort. Fortunately I had seen the picture for myself on that day in Canning Town; an experience which I never forgot or allowed out of my mind.

In my efforts to help those less fortunate than myself, whole classes of people showed their resentment to me in many ways,

10

singling me out for abuse. Consequently, although I had made thousands of friends in all parts of the country, I had made many enemies.

His criticism of Malvern College, perhaps of the system in general, may be a little harsh. It might be argued that young people went to Public Schools to learn academic subjects but not to be given a superiority complex or a social conscience. Parental influence at home might well be responsible for inculcating the latter, rather than the masters at school. There was no doubt, however, that the chance encounter in Canning Town with the denizens of a different world gave my uncle the conscience which was ever to fire his efforts to help those less fortunate than himself; efforts which were remembered by Sir Gerald Templer at Aldershot after his death.

It was the intention that he should try for a classical scholarship to Oxford but, having reached the Lower Sixth form, he surprised everybody by choosing to adopt the Army as his career. The reason for this sudden transfer was never clear to him, but was not as easy to achieve as it might seem at the time. Engrossed in so many outside activities, he had sacrificed some of the time which should have been devoted to books. Consequently, he failed the examination for the Royal Military College, Sandhurst, by quite a large margin. Thus he was sent to an 'army crammer' in London , an establishment run by the well-known Dr. Miller Maguire. The Public Schools concentrated, generally speaking, on Latin and Greek; useful for such professions as the Church, the Law and the Civil Service, but not required for the Army. Hence there was a special need to be 'crammed' in the subjects other than classics.

He was in good company. This much despised being, the army crammer, was responsible for many destined to be famous, including Sir Winston Churchill, General Sir Hubert Gough and Lord Kitchener. 'It was said that none but a congenital idiot could have avoided passing into Sandhurst,' wrote Winston in his *Early Life*.

But R.J.K. was in the particular company of a fellow Malvernian, J.F.C. Fuller, who had also failed the entrance exam. Fuller was later to become a Major General and a well-known military critic, the author of some 30 books on the subject. Both were unconventional men with firm ideas, and both respected each other during the coming years. Here, however, the affinity ended. Fuller, the more intellectual of the two, was interested in tactics and the art of war. A controversialist and an avid writer of papers, he pressed for the greater use of machine guns, artillery and – later – tanks, where Authority still worshipped the infanteer with his musket.

R.J.K., on the other hand, with a mania for sports and games – which Fuller abhorred – concentrated on the physical fitness of the soldier, morale and good leadership. Battles will be won, he argued, by those with the ball at their feet. Let the officer have his polo, but let him also lead his men to victory on the football field. In this way officer and man will get to know and respect each other. Leadership will fall into its natural place and morale will be high.

Dr Miller Maguire crammed my uncle with the answer to every kind of question he was liable to be asked. Away from home at the crucial moment he received a telegram from his father: 'You've passed into Sandhurst last but one, but, even so, our congratulations.' He was subsequently gazetted to Princess Victoria's Royal Irish Fusiliers (the old 87th and 89th Foot) in August 1897. Of his time at Sandhurst nothing is known.

3

The Presence of the Individual is Clearly Necessary

To appreciate what motivated R.J.K. during his soldiering days and later, it is necessary to take a look at the kind of Army into which he was gazetted in 1897. Prior to the Cardwell Reforms of 1881, Officers had to buy their commissions – and subsequent promotions – from the Government, so it might almost be said that the Army was private property. During the routine existence of peacetime garrison life the men carried out their daily drills, with, once a year, an expedition to the musketry camp, where they fired a small quantity of ammunition at fixed ranges. At any time after 11 a.m. the curtain rang down on further military activities. Those officers who were not on several months' leave took themselves off to hunt or to play polo – or to the Mess for a game of billiards. Thus it was that the future Lord Plumer, on joining his Regiment at Lucknow in 1877, could write home: 'The great game out here is polo. Everyone goes in for it.' If ever they had a twinge of conscience, they were bolstered up by the convenient philosophy that 'the machine was so perfect that the presence of the individual was unnecessary'.

What the soldier did with himself until 'Lights Out' was nobody's business, and nobody bothered. The Orderly Officer, perhaps, evinced a slight interest as he made a ceremonious tour of the men's barrack room – or, late at night, turned out to collect from the Wet Canteen that which had been so assiduously doled out at the previous pay parade.

After the Crimean War had been fought – to which some officers took their wives – it had occurred to many that it had not

13

been a conspicuous success, for all the bravery that had been shown. Between 1871 and 1881 sweeping reforms were carried out by Edward (later Lord) Cardwell in the teeth of vehement opposition from the Commander-In-Chief, the Duke of Cambridge. Promotion by purchase was abolished in favour of that by seniority – a system which effectively stifled talent but at least put officers on a much shorter rein than before.

But the old Army took a long time to die. Lord Wolseley crossed swords with the Duke of Cambridge much later by publishing his provocative *Soldiers Notebook* containing his famous 'Maxims', so thoroughly made use of by R.J.K. in 1915. This enunciated, in effect, that battles would not, and could not, be won unless the officers knew their men and vice versa – the presence of the individual, in fact, was clearly necessary! Paradoxically, of course, it was during the Queen's reign that this country had amassed the greatest Empire of all time. Besides foxes, pheasants and polo balls, the British officer (and his men) had, whilst on active service, chased almost every other kind of living thing on earth: Zulus, Hottentots, Chinese, Arabs, Dervishes, Mussulmen, Kurds, Egyptians, Maoris and Bantus, to name only a few. But, in 1899, the formerly impregnable Army came up against the most formidable antagonist that ever crossed the path of Imperial Britain – the rough, hard-bitten Boer farmers with their inconveniently modern rifles and the very latest in heavy artillery.

Lord Roberts, who had been sent from Ireland to South Africa after the initial disasters, heard his Chief of Staff, Kitchener, complain that the war was looked on as a 'game of polo with intervals for afternoon tea'. After dismissing 28 Officers, most of them cavalrymen, Lord Roberts reversed the situation and saved the day. He, at any rate, was determined that, on this occasion, at least, no dignity was to be lent to what might turn out to be an unseemly brawl!

This was the situation that R.J.K. first experienced; and, at the age of 23, he was disillusioned. After the Boer War was over the realization came, as after the Crimean War, that all was not well. It had been a salutory lesson and a shock to more than a few. Among the shocked was Lieutenant (later Major General) R.C. Fuller, whose Regiment, after two years of commando warfare in the

Veldt, had returned to the same old drills and musketry. He was pleased, nevertheless, that young officers were beginning to take an interest in the basic rudiments of war and even leaving their regiment to do a course at the Staff College at Camberley.

R.J.K, whilst not belittling this new outlook, was convinced that the soldier had got to spend his leisure time actively taking part in sports and games instead of drinking vast quantities of beer and sleeping off the results on his bed during the afternoon. As matters stood, he reckoned that the British soldier prior to 1910 was not physically fit enough to stand up to the army of a first-class European power. The burning question, for him, was where all these sports and games were to take place, for no grounds – or very few – existed for the purpose. It was in this setting that he eventually persuaded the GOC-in-C, Aldershot, to let each unit build its own playing fields with himself, a young Captain, in charge of operations.

Kentish and Fuller were, perhaps, complementary to each other. If we had failed, however, to realize the importance of machine guns and artillery by 1914, we had largely assured that the once bored soldier was beginning to eschew the delights of beer and women in favour of healthier pursuits. *Mens sana in corpore sano.*

R.J.K. was gazetted to Princess Victoria's Royal Irish Fusiliers in August 1897 and posted to the 1st Battalion (the old 87th), then recently arrived in Burma after a tour of service in India. Until such time as it arrived in Egypt he was attached to the 2nd Battalion (the old 89th), then in Colchester under Lieutenant Colonel John Reeves, 'a giant of a man with a giant of a voice and a giant of an appetite'. There he spent six months, mostly, to his disgust 'on the square', sloping, shouldering, ordering, present-ing, trailing and securing arms to the point of nausea under the Adjutant, Captain Colin Dick. In 1898 he set sail for Alexandria, where the 1st Battalion was now stationed in Mustapha Barracks, Sidi Gabr.

He thought the men were 'magnificent, just giants and created an equally magnificent appearance on parade. But, unfortunately, they had the habit of drinking 15 pints of beer on paydays.' A day or so after his arrival Barrosa Day was celebrated. A précis of his own account follows:

15

The day was ushered in with musical honours, after which everything was done to give the men the best time possible. Regimental Sports were held on the Battalion parade ground in the afternoon, and then followed the Barrosa Dinner in the Officers' Mess. About 60 sat down in the dining room, the walls of which were covered with the heads of every kind of animal shot during service in India and Burma. On a side table, flanked by two Burmese drums, was the huge foot of an elephant, hollowed out and used as a waste-paper basket.

I don't suppose, if you had entered a Ducal Palace, you would have seen anything more magnificent than the Mess Staff and their full Mess Livery, a green cutaway coat, scarlet waistcoat, green plush breeches with gold knee bands, white stockings, black shoes with gold buckles and – powdered hair!

Hardly had we sat down at the table, ornamented with gold and silver plate, separated by gorgeously coloured flowers, than, 'mirabile dictu', there was a set-to on the floor between Jimmy Wilson and Philip Gould, both of whom were enamoured with a certain lady, who had given her attention that afternoon to one rather than the other! The Adjutant, Dick Rice, however, hauled them up by the scruff of their necks and little damage was done. Then came amazing incident No. 2. After the Queen's health had been drunk there appeared on the top, and at the far end, of the table, the 'wicked baronet' – Sir Henry Hill. There he was – I can see him now in his perfectly fitting mess kit – moving with the grace and poise of a ballet dancer down the table, never touching a single glass, and there must have been nearly 200 on the table, as he passed along to the strains of the band!.

And now amazing incident No. 3. Without any warning I saw first one Officer, then the one on his right, slide very quickly from their chairs until their chins hit the table with a thud. Then I noticed that two more chairs were suddenly empty and so on down to the middle of the table where the Colonel, remarking that the human 'torpedoeists' were getting dangerously close, hurriedly withdrew from the table with the guests of honour. As I stood aside to let him pass I received a tremendous blow on the head. On regaining consciousness I was congratulated by Henry Holmes for stopping a chair which Gould, apparently bearing a grudge, had aimed at the Colonel. I was gratified to hear that Wilson had at once picked up the elephant's hoof and crashed it on Gould's head, inflicting an ugly wound.

The rest of the night can be left to the imagination. Suffice to say that R.J.K, unable to take any more, had slipped, unobtrusively as he thought, to his bungalow, from whence he, the junior wart, was hunted, declothed, and laid stark naked on the Mess floor. 'The heart of the Senior Subaltern must have suddenly softened,' thought R.J.K., 'for he ordered me to be wrapped in a tablecloth and taken back to my quarters, admonishing me severely for leaving before all the guests had departed.'

* * * * *

Four months later there occurred the second incident which was to leave a vivid impression on my uncle. He had seen the undernourished youth of London trying to play football on Beckton Marshes; now he was to experience the effect which poor leadership could have on men of fine physique and *esprit-de-corps,* men from the country districts of Ireland.

Only fools delude themselves that 'famous Regiments' are always tuned to the highest pitch. In 1898, my uncle reckoned, the Battalion, after years of inactive service in sultry and unhealthy climates, had, in spite of the magnificent material available, sunk into a state of semi-stupor and was living on its fat gained during the Napoleonic Wars.

In July of that year, however, much to everyone's delight, the Battalion received orders to proceed to Cairo to join the Brigade which was to reinforce Sir Herbert Kitchener in his attempt to reconquer the Sudan. Unfortunately, the departure time from Sidi Gabr railway station was long after the Wet Canteen had been opened in the barracks. As assistant entraining officer, my uncle saw what looked like 'a huge serpent coming down the road, with one part of its body on one side and now on the other.' Soldiers have been inebriated before and will doubtless be so again, but this particular occasion was crowned by the arrival of a Private Coyle of 'H' Company, who had escaped from the hospital, where he was also a prisoner. In full view of the Governor of Alexandria, the GOC troops and the assembled ladies, Private Coyle could be seen on the bridge connecting the two platforms wearing nothing but his birthday suit and a khaki helmet! 'Sure and you'll not be leaving me behind ye! Bejaysus! Oi'm comin'wid yer. Be God, I am!'

On reaching Cairo the Battalion marched out to a camp at Mena House, where it was to carry out a week's training with the rest of the Brigade. Here, amongst other manoeuvres, it had to practise 'forming square' in preparation for an attack by the mounted dervishes to be found in the Sudan. But it soon became apparent that there was much criticism in the air and that the senior Officers were *persona non grata* with the General. The upshot of this was that the Battalion was returned from whence it had come and another regiment was brought over from Malta to take its place.

This was a bitter blow to the young officers and the men, as it was also to those at the top, who suffered from the bristles of the brush which swept them clean away. 'But,' as R.J.K. wrote, 'out of evil sometimes cometh good. This incident had a far-reaching effect.' After a slow start the Battalion picked up until, by 1914, it was a paragon of virtue in all fields of endeavour, since when it has never looked back.

Starting afresh, the Battalion, under more inspiring leadership, turned once again to its garrison existence at Sidi Gabr – polo, racing, shooting – and drill! Occasionally R.J.K. had to go out on detachment, which he very much disliked since he had to arrange his own messing. This was not an easy thing to do on the £7 or so which Her Majesty then gave monthly to young subalterns. Tailors could wait – and did wait – but mess bills had to be paid. He never had any idea of the value of money. He did know, however, or he thought he knew, that some inefficient man called Cox (King had not then appeared) was robbing him of half what he was entitled to. He also knew that, should a tall enough story be told, a kindly father would generally come to his help if in difficulties.

His letters home, long but infrequent, nearly always contained an account – perhaps for father's benefit – of Arabs who raided the quarters and stole clothes, binoculars or firearms. One account, at least, is probably true. 'On returning to my room I saw a blooming Arab chuck down a bundle and fly. I've never seen a fellow run like he did. I chased him past the Mess, panting to some men to join me, which one of them did.' (This man, McGovern, was one of the powdered gentleman whom we met on Barrosa night.) 'Like the faithful hound that he was, he answered his master's horn and, with the cry, "Begorrah, it's Mr Kentish after a thafe," he joined in the hunt. We ran the villain off his legs about half a mile from, and in view of, the Mess. The bundle he had dropped contained all my mufti coats to the number of 12.' Father got off lightly this time, but not so the 'thafe' by the time that several Fusiliers had finished with him!

In May, 1899, R.J.K. travelled to Cairo to take his exam for promotion to Lieutenant. This consisted of drilling a company and then a battalion. Having passed this severe test of military knowledge he then returned to Alexandria to attend the Khedive's Ball. 'He shook hands with us all,' he wrote home, 'and said he was very glad to see me. I replied that I was very glad to see him and hoped that he would have a good dance, and that if he wanted a partner or two I could put him on to some good ones. After leaving at 3.15 a.m., we had to drive six miles to Mustapha Barracks; then we had to get up for a route march at 5 a.m. – which was a bit thick.'

There had been quite a fracas at the ball. At supper time the Khedive had retired to a private room, taking with him the wives of the foreign Consuls. The English Consul and others had shown indifference to the possible fate awaiting the ladies, but not so the German, the Frenchman and the Austrian, who, bearing down on the Arab Master of Ceremonies outside the door, demanded entrance – which was refused. Growing violent, they so frightened him that he was forced to let them through, and the rescued spouses were marched straight out of the Palace. 'An inquiry is to be held,' wrote R.J.K., 'as a result of which apologies will have to be tendered by one side or the other; but I am glad that our own Consul, Gould, had no part in the commotion.'

4

President Kruger's Guest in Pretoria

The Boer War in South Africa broke out in October 1899 and ended in 1902 after the Imperial and Colonial armies had suffered about 450,000 casualties of all kinds. It was the first time the British had come up against forces other than, for example, Dervishes and Bantus, since the Crimean War. The fight against President Kruger and the Boers, who were settled in the Transvaal and Orange Free State, was looked on as an imperialist aggression by other Great Powers, and with a certain amount of reserve in British official circles. Kruger could put 50,000 men into the field – not men, like the British, who deemed it a disgrace to lie down on the ground, but well-trained marksmen who darted from cover to cover, forming invisible targets.

Expected to be 'over by Christmas', the war dragged on for three years. The Irish Fusiliers, still stationed at Alexandria, were immediately sent to reinforce the meagre British garrison of 10,000 in Natal and Cape Colony. R.J.K. wrote several long letters to his parents, mainly, it would seem, to hint that father might send a generous cheque to reimburse the cost of the necessary extra items of kit required – and later for the loss of full dress, scarlet tunic and bearskin, etc., which had so unnecessarily fallen into the hands of the Boers.

Sidi Gabr, 23 September, 1899

> Just about to start on service and we are all very jubilant. It looks
> like war. We are only allowed to take three bags, and when we get

20

to Durban can only take 35 lb of kit up. I have been awfully busy buying service kit – and it has been a trifle costly.

The SS *Avoca* set sail via the Suez Canal for Durban. Whilst steaming through the Red Sea a boat drill was held. There were 1200 souls on board, but only room for 800 in the boats. The proceedings only interested those who were 'told off' to be saved. There was little enthusiasm for the parade shown by the unfortunate 400 who had to stand to attention and sing 'God Save The Queen' if and when the ship went down.

SS *Avoca*, Aden, 30 September, 1899

We embarked on the 24th. The men presented a very fine appearance, and we have all got green patches on each side of our helmets. The 'Horse Guards' have just presented us with a green hackle which we shall wear on our bearskins at home. They will look very pretty .... I think the Boers are awful idiots to fight although, of course, we are very keen that they should from our point of view. I have got a very serviceable kit for the field, but it has cost me a good deal and we lose a good deal in allowances going from Egypt. But what we lose in money we hope to make up for in honour and glory. I expect it will be a fairly sharp fight while it lasts – mostly Artillery versus Artillery. They have an army of about 50,000 men and are not to be despised at all ... General Talbot, Commanding Troops in Egypt, came to see us off and said he could hardly believe that there was such a fine battalion: the men looked really magnificent ... I have written to Cox's and have asked them to refer to you if I am overdrawn ...

Port Natal, 12 October, 1899

We have just reached Durban and hear that Kruger has presented an ultimatum to our troops to withdraw from the frontier. This expired yesterday and Sir George White and his staff left Durban at once for Ladysmith. I hope I come through all right. I have a very complete kit and am in a low state of finance. I am taking with me my Wolseley Valise and a kit weighing 40 lb, whilst on me I carry waterproof, sword, revolver, haversack, flask, drinking cup, water bottle, whistle, money belt (with no money in it), socks, vest, cholera belt, flannel shirt and an oyster shell over my heart to keep the bullets out. We hope to be lunching at the White Hart, Pretoria, in about a month's time, Kruger having asked the 'Faughs'* to an 'al fresco' meal. I shall take every precaution to get behind rocks and boulders, great boulders for choice . . . I don't expect the Boers will have a chance, although I expect there will be one or two stiff little shows here and there.

Thus, full of enthusiasm, R.J.K. and the 1st Battalion arrived in the country that was to be their home for nearly three years. Kitchener thought that the war was conducted as a game of polo with intervals with afternoon tea. With other units, the 'Faughs' were to take part in two tea intervals: the Boers, unfortunately, forgot to stop on the second occasion. True to R.J.K.'s prognostications, the Battalion was a guest of Kruger in Pretoria within a month of landing – but the occasion was far from al fresco. Against these rough farmers, each with his rifle and his horse, superb parade ground drill was not good enough – however magnificent the human material.

No sooner had the Faughs disembarked at Durban, where they were given a tumultuous reception, than they were despatched north to Ladysmith, where Sir George White, VC, had taken over command of about 8,000 men, with another 4,000 at Dundee and Glencoe to safeguard the railway and the collieries there. From this area Sir George hoped to deal with the Boers debouching from the Transvaal and Orange Colony to the North and West.

On arrival, the Faughs immediately took over the outposts round the town. R.J.K. wrote:

Sir George White had taken his force out early that morning to carry out a reconnaissance to try to contact the Boers. That same afternoon we heard music and, looking out in the direction taken by our Force, we saw much to our surprise, a band, with the sun flashing on their instruments, marching at the head of the returning troops and blowing for all they were worth, with Sir George White riding at their head! I relate this incident because it was amazing

---

*'Faughs' was the Regimental nickname from its motto, 'Faugh a Ballagh', meaning 'clear the way'.

that we should see and hear a brass band, the men blowing like the devil as they stepped out across the Veldt! Thus did we go to, and return from, battle in those days!

After two days we went up to Dundee and Glencoe, about 40 miles to the north-east of Ladysmith. What made Sir George White split his force into two and why he did not make a stand on the line of the Tugela, in the south, I shall never understand.

I shall always remember our little camp at Glencoe with its row after row of white bell tents – white, if you please, to tell the enemy exactly where we were so that they could range their guns on us from the surrounding heights. This and the brass band incident seemed to me most incongruous!

When asked what would happen if he woke up one morning and found the Boers on Talana Hill or Impali (two of the overlooking heights), the Force Commander, General Symons, replied: 'Why, attack them at once, of course.' The inevitable happened: the Boers occupied Talana Hill and ranged their guns on to the rows of white tents at Glencoe. The opening rounds of the War had been fired. As the Boer, Denis Reytz, wrote afterwards, 'We were so dumbfounded at finding Talana Hill unoccupied on our arrival that nobody, for some considerable time, knew what to do next.'

The attack on the steep-sided Talana heights by the British soldier against an unknown enemy and after inadequate reconnaissance or preparation is almost an epic. The artillery had opened up on Glencoe just after Stand-to at 4.45 a.m. and the issue of 'gunfire', as the early morning tea was called; only on this day there was a double dose. Orders were rapped out and shortly afterwards the Leicesters, 60th Rifles, Faughs and other arms were advancing, in skirmishing order, towards the steep slopes of Talana, with orders from General Penn Symons to clear the enemy from the top. The idea was to take advantage of a wood halfway up and a piece of grazing ground surrounded by a stone wall. No precise instructions having been given as to the method, the Brigade clambered up as best it could, taking advantage of an early mist. The summit was reached by the leading waves only to find wounded, dead and general disorder.

It was then that R.J.K., who was commanding his Company after the wound inflicted on Capt. George Southey and who was slightly behind the crest, saw, coming towards him, a couple of mounted men, one carrying a white flag. He wrote:

> Running forward, I came up to them and they handed me a piece of paper folded in two, which I read. It humbly begged for an armistice to bury the dead and carry away the wounded: it was signed 'Lucas Meyer, Commanding Boer Forces'. Telling the two men to dismount I had them blindfolded and led back to our head-quarters; whereupon I called upon my men to advance to the top of the hill. There, stretched across the plain on the other side, were hundreds of mounted men going as hard as they could – a perfect target for our artillery, and well indeed had they begun to do their job. Then suddenly there came the sound of bugles, first one, then the other, blowing the 'Cease Fire'. The two Boers had been taken to General Yule (the Force Commander, General Symons, had been mortally wounded whilst riding about preceded by a red pennant), who, after consultation with his Staff, had agreed to the armistice.
>
> But, instead of standing their ground whilst the dead and wounded were looked after, the Boers had legged it as fast as they could. There was no cavalry pursuit and we were thus deprived of the fruits of victory after having carried out a brilliant and gallant storming of the Boer position.
>
> In the evening we returned to our Camp – bell tents again – in Glencoe. Fighting had begun at 5.30 a.m. and finished at 2.30 p.m. The men, who had had nothing to eat from Tea on Thursday to Tea on Friday, fought brilliantly with the pluck of the devil. Rain poured down in torrents and they marched back to camp full of spirits and cheered by the townspeople.

By the next day, Saturday, 21 October, the Brigade Group was in a perilous position. The Boers had cut the railway line to Ladysmith, had occupied the Impali heights and had opened up on Dundee with siege guns, firing with great accuracy, to which our own field guns could not reply. On Sunday, news got through from Ladysmith that the Boers had been heavily defeated at Elandslaagte and the enemy subsequently withdrew from Impali. It had rained for 48 hours, and the troops had had scarcely a bite for 24. A withdrawal to Ladysmith was planned for 10 p.m. on the Sunday evening, by a roundabout route of 60 miles. The Battalion, never having been issued with Regimental transport, had to abandon its heavy baggage and property, which included band instruments, £200 worth of Mess stores and bottles of champagne – the last destined for the peace celebrations.

After the three-mile column had passed within 1,000 yards of the Boers, and after suffering many vicissitudes in the way of thunderstorms and short rations, the Brigade entered Ladysmith on Thursday, 26 October, where the Manchesters looked after the Faughs until their tents had been erected. R.J.K. wrote:

> I fancy that Regiment saw the Faughs at their best as regards sleeping and eating. We stood up in our worldly possessions, except a few of us who had left a box or two at Ladysmith. I had lost my valise, kit bag, service kit, camp equipment, saddlery and a large box containing full dress and blue serge. The Boers had looted the train which was bringing our heavy kit up from Durban – why it was sent God only knows – and were actually wearing our things when taken prisoner at Elandslaagte.

After breakfast on Friday, the Battalion, after only one night's sleep, was re-brigaded and went off under General Ian Hamilton to Modders Spruit to prevent a force of Boers cutting the line back to Durban. An attack was ordered from dawn on Saturday, with the Faughs in the lead. R.J.K. wrote:

> We were all very jubilant and thought it was a splendid opportunity for the Regiment, but we were told that Sir George White thought it too risky an experiment. So we all retired back to Ladysmith, very sick at not having a go at the devils. That afternoon I had 10 days growth of beard removed but failed to get a bath. It is unlikely that the Boers will attack tomorrow as they do not like fighting on Sundays.

On Sunday, however, Sir White hatched another plot. To disorganize the Boers who were closing in on Ladysmith from the west, north and east, he decided that his force, roughly three Brigades of Infantry, a Brigade of Cavalry and the Artillery, should sally forth on Monday morning, 30 October, and attack them. On the night before, however, after dark, a small force under Colonel Carleton was to pass through the enemy positions to the north and take up a position on Nicholson's Nek, a high plateau one mile long by a quarter of a mile wide, so that it might give the retreating Boers a warm reception on the next day.

A précis of R.J.K.'s account of the battle and how he came to be a guest of Kruger in Pretoria is prefaced by the thought that being taken a prisoner-of-war is a subject a soldier is anxious to forget.

On Sunday night, October 29, Carleton's column moved out silently after dark, passing within a quarter of a mile of the Boer positions without a shot being fired. I was marching at the rear of my Company, the last in the Battalion. Behind me came the Gloucesters; then the 10th Mountain Battery with their guns on mules. In addition each Company had its own mules for ammunition and signalling equipment: this made a total of about 200 mules.

We had just turned left up the track leading to Nicholson's Nek when some shots rang out, accompanied by the clattering of horses's hooves ahead of us, probably a Boer patrol. In two minutes the mules at the head of the column lashed out, broke loose and came careering down the line. The panic spread until every one of them, those with the guns included, had disappeared into the darkness. I remember being thrown flat on my back as they thundered past. Half an hour after the stampede we started off back up the steep track leading to Nicholson's Nek, where we lay until daybreak when we took up our positions: the Gloucesters to the West of the hill and ourselves to the East. From here we could see our mules on the plain below, some being caught by the Boers, some going on back to Ladysmith.

The second phase of this extraordinary battle began when we saw the glittering bayonets of our troops advancing from Ladysmith to drive the Boers into our positions but the enemy opened up a sustained fire with 40 and 96 pounders, against which our 15 pounders could not reply. We tried to get in touch with Sir George White by helio, using biscuit tins, to tell him of our predicament: then a Kaffir volunteered to take a message back – but all in vain. By 12 noon all firing on the main front had ceased: Sir George White fearing a breakthrough in the centre, had ordered all troops back to Ladysmith; so ended the battle!

The Boers, meanwhile, had turned their attention on to us, and, in an hour or so, orders were given to attack the '*verdammte*

Roineks'. A heavy attack developed against the Gloucesters, some of whom had to fall back, leaving their Company Commander mortally wounded. After about three hours of firing our ammunition was running short and the isolated officer, thinking he was all alone and that everyone had left the Nek, ordered a man with him to show a white handkerchief. This started the rot and allowed the Boers to get right into our positions. I was just applying a tourniquet to my wounded Company Commander, Silver, with no thoughts of surrender – we were virtually intact except for ammunition – when I suddenly heard, 'Hands oop!', and looking up I saw a dozen wild looking fellows with beards pointing Mausers at me. Then I saw them everywhere, with our men surrendering – they had no alternative. So ended the Battle of Nicholson's Nek, a tragedy from start to finish. Without passing judgement, adverse or otherwise, on the white handkerchief incident, I can only say that our own men had absolutely nothing to do with it.

From the mountain we were taken down to Joubert's HQ under guard of the Irish Brigade – every one of them an Irish rebel fighting for Kruger against the Queen – and this was the unkindest cut of all. From there we marched, and finally entrained, to Pretoria, the Capital of the Transvaal.

My uncle's opinion was that Colonel Carleton, despite the loss of ammunition and guns, had been right to stay on the Nek. They had been under fire for nine hours, for the last three of which they had carried out a musketry duel with those Boers who had penetrated the position. But the enemy's skill at sharpshooting had been too much for the British, who had only been trained to fire at fixed ranges.

* * * * * *

The camp in Pretoria where officers were incarcerated with their soldier servants was a one-storeyed school building containing about 12 large classrooms, standing in a playground 120 yards square, surrounded on two sides by an iron grille and on two by a corrugated iron fence, 10 feet high. There were three sentries inside and six out.

November 9, 1899.

I feel more like a schoolgirl having her letters read than a soldier ... I will describe to you our daily life. After being pestered during the night by mosquitoes we are woken at 6 a.m. by the flies. At 6.30 tea is brought round by the soldier servants: after a bath, then breakfast at 8 a.m. Lunch is at 10, after which we walk about or sleep until 4.30 p.m. Dinner, the best meal of the day, is at 7. The Transvaal Government provides a daily ration and the mess can buy anything it likes, except alcohol, from the town; a cheque drawn on Cox & Co., being accepted as good legal tender!

What we really have to complain about is the question of parole. Even if they will not send us home, they might at least let us walk about outside. Our only form of exercise here is confined to the playground, and I venture to think that the most retired matron of doubtful summers would soon be fed up with this form of amusement.

The Boers have provided us with beds and a complete set of bedding. We were also presented with about 52 suits, 'off the peg', 'reach-me-downs', of all colours and sizes. I managed to secure a fair fit of stylish chocolate trousering varied by a coat of brown holland. I made a tie out of a lady's skirt which I found on the way up here in a looted train. We also have pyjamas and carpet slippers and I have bought washing things and got rid of my villainous beard.

I cannot conceive why we are not allowed newspapers of any description nor allowed to visit our men, about a mile away ... I have the consolation of knowing that I took part in by far the most brilliant achievement of British Soldiers in modern days at Talana Hill, showing the public what our Regiment could do before taking part in the eventual engagement on October 31.

November 26, 1899

Have been very seedy for the last two weeks when I was brought into the hospital here, a building in the school grounds, suffering from typhoid fever caused by drinking the foul water on the march from Dundee to Ladysmith.

December 15, 1899

Am glad to hear the papers do not judge us too harshly ... I am nothing but a bag of bones and am fed on tea, custard and jellies.

December 27, 1899

Just beginning the 7th week of my illness but thanks to the kindness of the staff am well on the way to recovery. Having told the doctor (an Irishman) that I was hanging up my stocking for a chicken, he let me have my solid food in the shape of a breast – but no turkey or plum pudding, thank you! The Officers next door had a great feed on Christmas Day. Their numbers have nearly doubled now. Father de Lacey, a Catholic Priest here, very kindly got up a subscription for getting our men a Christmas dinner and managed to send 4 oxen, 50 sheep, 50 lb of tobacco and 2,000 clay pipes. I was delighted as I had been thinking about the men's dinner for a long time. Winston Churchill's escape from here about a fortnight ago has made a lot of difference to the treatment of those next door and they have to answer their names twice a day.

Winston Churchill, War Correspondent to the *Morning Post,* had been taken prisoner from an armoured train and brought to Pretoria in early December. For three weeks or so he continued to aggravate the Boer government until he escaped by scaling the 10-foot fence after dark. The flight caused a major sensation in the Transvaal. The Boer authorities, leaving no stone unturned, insisted on searching R.J.K.'s bed, both in and under, despite the Matron's protestations that it only contained a dying man who should be left in peace.

February 23, 1900

Am now quite fit and have been out of hospital three weeks .... Life is dreary and monotonous in the extreme.

April 14,1900

There are nearly 140 of us in here now. Five fellows tried to escape the other night. I was playing cards when a loud bang was followed by three more. No one was hurt and no one got away.

I would give all I possess to be exchanged and I'll take my oath that I'd never be taken prisoner again. Of all the abominable, dreary, monotonous, depressing ways of passing one's life, this is far and away the worst...

The Government will be responsible for my lost kit in so far as paying me a probable £50 is concerned, but when I consider that my losses cannot be far short of £500 this is little solace. When we heard, on arrival back in Ladysmith, that our heavy kit had been captured on its way up from Durban to Dundee, we were dumb-founded. Whoever gave the order for sending such things as chests of drawers, wash-hand stands and cases containing full dress and mufti up to Dundee must be a lunatic.

I have so far received 68 letters, including one from Miss Freeland of the Cheltenham Girls' High School, and a 'tract' from a lady in Cork, requesting me to read it. Why I am singled out for this favour is beyond me.

On 6 June 1900, Pretoria was taken by Lord Roberts. R.J.K. wrote:

For the past week, there had been a stream of Boers past our camp, all fleeing from the hated '*Roineks*'. A very wild, sullen looking crowd they were and our Commandant had warned us to keep out of sight. but on June 7 there had been no movement at all, and, at any moment, we expected to see our own troops in pursuit. Arnold Burrowes and I had determined that, at the moment of our release, we should replace the Boer flag outside the guardhouse with a Union Jack which Burrowes had cleverly made with a needle and concealed about his body.

As we stood talking near the main gate we saw a couple of horsemen coming galloping up, and to our surprise recognised Winston Churchill, who had made such a dramatic escape in December. Greeting us, and introducing his cousin, the Duke of Marlborough, he ordered the sentry to open the gates, an order immediately complied with. Out we dashed to the flagstaff, up which, with Burrowes' help, I climbed and replaced the Boer flag with our own. And I remember well that, as I touched mother earth again, Winston Churchill came up and said: 'Will you let me have that flag? I'll give you a fiver, or anything else you like for it!' 'I'm sorry', I said, 'but it belongs to my Regiment.' 'Right O,' he replied and off we went to the camp to collect our kit.

Thus ended our captivity, and the last time I saw our guards they were being put inside the camp with our soldier servants mounting guard over them outside the gates!

* * * * *

Although the war was officially over by June, 1900, and the Transvaal and Orange River Colony officially annexed, sporadic

30

fighting was to continue for nearly two years, with the Boers carrying out guerrilla or commando raids, particularly on our communications by rail down to Durban and Capetown. To combat this, garrisons were established down the lines, with mobile columns operating into the surrounding countryside.

After his release in June, 1900, it would appear that R.J.K went home on several months' sick leave until February 1901. From the following July, until the end of the war in 1902, he was in command of some 100 Faughs who formed a special Mounted Infantry Detachment under the command of the Edenburg Garrison in the Orange River Colony. His duties were to carry out sorties on his own, but he was obliged, if necessary, to work in with any of the larger independent columns operating temporarily in the area. The following story may not only illustrate these duties but give some insight into his character.

Having returned to Edenburg after several nights in the Veldt, he and his men were immediately ordered out again to escort some supplies to the Rawlinson Column, which had just encamped for rest some 10 miles away. Having done this, he was to collect as many cattle and ploughs as he could find. (Colonel Sir Henry Rawlinson, later to be C-in-C, 4th Army, in France in the First World War and then C-in-C, India, was at that time, the 'Blue-eyed boy' of Kitchener, then Commander-in-Chief.) So, having delivered the rations, R.J.K. was setting off for Redburg when Rawlinson's Staff Officer accosted him with orders that, as the column was tired, R.J.K.'s men should take over the outposts for the night. Bearing in mind that his own men were just as tired, my uncle complained that he came under the command of the Edenburg garrison, but, after uttering some well-chosen and expletive oaths against Rawlinson, was forced to comply.

The following morning, when preparing to depart from the Camp, he was ordered to appear before Rawlinson himself, whom he found sitting at a table in his office tent. 'So you are the impertinent young officer who dared to cavil at my orders last night,' said the Great Man, 'what is your name?' 'Kentish, Sir,' said my uncle, giving what he called his Number One Salute.

'Well, Kentish,' ended Rawlinson, after giving him a thorough dressing down, 'if ever you should come up before me in later years for advancement or promotion, I shall do this.' And, tearing up the piece of paper on which he had previously written my uncle's name into little pieces, he threw them angrily into the waste-paper basket. 'And that,' he added finally, 'will be the end of Kentish!'

The sequel occurred some months later. My father, having just been gazetted to the Royal Fusiliers, was sent out to South Africa with a RF Mounted Infantry Company under command of Captain Guy du Maurier, which Company was sent, on arrival, to join the Rawlinson Column.

R.J.K., still at Edenburg, eventually received a letter from his brother – the two resembled each other after a fashion – enquiring as to whether he had ever come up against Rawlinson at some time or other. My father wrote:

Our Column was returning to base one day when Du Maurier ordered me to take a cart ahead to a certain store to replenish stocks for our Mess. Having loaded up the cart with whatever I could lay hands on, who should come riding up with his retinue but 'Rawly', evidently bent on the same mission as myself! On seeing me he had a hurried word with his Staff Officer, then, coming over, said: 'So it's the impertinent young Officer again! What are you doing here?' 'W-well, Sir,' I began (my father had a slight stutter). 'I don't want any Wells,' replied 'Rawly', 'put all that back again and rejoin the Column at once.'

My Company Commander eventually took the blame on his shoulders and 'Rawly' also apologised for the mistaken identity, so all was well.

5

The Birth of An Idea

After the South African War it was again apparent, as after the Crimean War, that bravery and good drill were hardly good enough, and would not be good enough, against professional armies such as those the French, Germans and Austro-Hungarians had built up and used against each other in the preceding century. A battle must no longer be looked on as a sport, or kind of field day, against semi-civilized or badly-armed tribesmen; there had to be a motivation other than a quest for honour and glory.

Poorly paid and neglected though he always had been, there was little wrong with the British soldier when it came to a fight; he had proved his worth over and over again, particularly when fighting against overwhelming odds, or when trained by great commanders such as Marlborough, Moore or Napier. The trouble lay in the fact that officers had never been trained seriously to conduct war on a higher level than a Brigade. There were no Field Service Regulations, nor had Principles of War ever been formulated. An officer in the infantry who wished to try for the Staff College was looked on as a crank, and liable to be asked whether his Regiment was not good enough for him.

The Haldane Reforms, however, introduced in 1908, provided the base on which the new professional army was to grow; an army – the finest since the New Model Army of Cromwell's day – which was eventually to withstand the German onslaughts at Mons and Le Cateau in 1914. Not only was an effort to be made to concentrate more on field training and tactics, but steps were to be taken to cater for the physical needs and welfare of the new type of short-service soldier – a man of rather different calibre to his predecessor of 1870 and before. The relationship between officer and man was to be radically altered now that the savage discipline of former days had been dispensed with.

In this transformation the 1st Battalion played a conspicuous and creditable part. Starting in 1902 with a reputation that was below par, it had emerged by 1910 as a Battalion that was to be feared for its prowess and envied for its *esprit de corps*. Through being held up to others as an example, it was to become the most disliked unit in the Aldershot Command. It is difficult to say who, if indeed it was any one individual, was responsible for this, but a good share can certainly be apportioned to R.J.K., with his infectious enthusiasm and his ideas that were more than revolutionary to the older generation of soldiers.

After 20 years of foreign service, the 1st Battalion returned from South Africa in 1902 and was sent to Holywood Barracks in Belfast. This was some two decades before Ireland was to be partitioned into Ulster (or Northern Ireland) and the Irish Free State (Eire). R.J.K. noted:

> Among a group of friends on the quayside was the Bandmaster A.J. Dunn. Andy Dunn, the Bandmaster of the Battalion from 1898 to 1918, was indeed one of those who were going to bring the Regiment to fame, and a very real friend he was. Armed only with swords in brass-tipped scabbards he and his men had played a gallant part in the attack on Talana Hill in 1899. After the subsequent retirement from Dundee all instruments had had to be abandoned, and the Bandmaster had last been seen when the Battalion crept out of Ladysmith to take part in the unfortunate episode at Nicholson's Nek. For the remainder of the war he had been in Ireland, training a new and young band which was now present on the quayside to play the men ashore.

Andy Dunn and his bandsmen made their debut in Ulster Hall in Belfast. There, a young boy, later to be an officer in the Regiment, noted the arrival of parties of officers, who had been driven over from Holywood in horse brakes, taking up their seats reserved for them by two soldiers in red tunics. The fame of the band spread to other concert halls and to seaside resorts and, no matter whether it was playing topical airs, military marches or classical pieces, the bandmaster conducted without a note of music in front of him. At Aldershot the populace came to watch the Battalion marching back from church, and King Edward, referring to the band, is alleged to have remarked, on one occasion, 'Just as good as my Guards!' The bandmaster was duly fitted out with a frock coat, a refinement normally only reserved for officers, and the remainder of the Line Regiments eventually copied the innovation.

* * * * *

After being at Holywood for four years, the Battalion left for Dublin in early 1906 to join the 13th (Dublin) Infantry Brigade. In those days the 5th and 6th Divisions and a Cavalry Brigade were quartered in Ireland. My uncle at this time was Adjutant – he had held the appointment since December 1904 – to Lt.-Col. (later Brigadier-General) Felix Hill, 'one of the best COs the Regiment has ever had'. From this remark it can be gauged that the two saw eye to eye!

In the preceding century the Adjutant, responsible for discipline, turnout and drill, had been a powerful figure. As a result of the Haldane Reforms of 1908 field training was to play a more important part in the soldiers' daily life, yet the Adjutant retained his influence until the introduction of mechanized transport relegated him more and more to the Orderly Room and paper work. Stories about R.J.K. have now passed into legend. Whether, adopting the Churchillian touch, he really gave out his orders lying in a bath with a cigar in his mouth is a matter for conjecture – but he certainly made himself felt.

Drill and turn-out were excellent; discipline was severe, yet, in accordance with the new ideas, tempered with justice and common sense. The old idea that the soldier was an unthinking being who had to be kept in subjection by harsh punishment was now frowned on. In the partial absence of grounds for football, cricket and athletics, 'manly sports', such as cross-country running, bayonet fighting and tug-o-war, were indulged in with conspicuous success. Gaining a reputation for being 'somewhat different', the Battalion, much to the annoyance of the authorities, adopted certain peculiarities of dress. These customs prevailed in 1939, when officers of the Regiment, for instance, wore Guards pattern greatcoats and tunics (with a spine pad down the back), cavalry Sam Browne belts, and a shirt of colour and pattern of which only Hilditch & Key, of Jermyn Street, W1, could possibly have thought.

The Dublin Brigade was commanded by General C.C. Munro, whose regiment had been the Queen's Royal West Surreys, the old 2nd of Foot, of which the depot town was Guildford. And of this Regiment the General was peculiarly proud, so proud, in fact, that he never ceased to talk about it. Giving prior notice one day that he would like to inspect the latest recruits, he duly turned up on the parade ground, and, with a cheerful 'Good morning' to R.J.K., passed down the assembled ranks. As generals usually do, and are expected to do, he fired questions at the men as to their home towns, etc., and, having received a number of replies such as 'Dublin' or 'Monaghan', he came upon an obvious Englishman who said, 'Guildford, Sir.'

'Then why didn't you join the Queens' asked the General.

'Well, Sir,' said the man, confident that he was giving the correct answer, 'I never thought much of that lot, Sir, I wanted to join a real smart Regiment.'

The situation was Batemanesque, and the atmosphere electric. The Brigade-Major looked horrified, the Colonel turned hastily away and the RSM was poised as if to swallow the offending man wholesale. My uncle, of course, was delighted with this un-expected show of *esprit de corps,* but the General, giving Kent – for that was his name – a look of absolute contempt, passed down the line, and, with a quick 'Good morning', left the parade ground, having been bowled clean out by the recruit!

At some future date a request came from Brigade HQ for a chauffeur to drive the General's car. At that time a motor car was a very rare bird, but a soldier who could drive one was even rarer. It so happened that Kent was the only man in the Battalion who could do so. After confabulations at every level, the man was duly sent over to be given a trial.

Some little time later, when R.J.K. was having dinner with the Munros, Miss Munro, who kept house for her brother, said in the course of conversation, 'Charlie is so pleased with Kent, he's a real find. Not only does he drive the car well but he is so useful about the house, especially in the kitchen. So handy that we have been able to dispense with our kitchen maid.'

'I am so glad,' said R.J.K., but felt inwardly concerned, for he knew that the General's cook, who happened to be a Greek girl, was a particularly good-looking woman. He thought no more about it until, when returning to barracks one evening, he noticed men hanging out of their windows watching a cloud of dust in the square, in the middle of which was Kent in the General's car, giving an exhibition of trick driving, now flying round in ever-smaller concentric circles, now zigzagging this way and that.

The next day, when my uncle was preparing to ring Brigade HQ about the previous evening's indiscipline, the Brigade-Major himself rang to say that not only was Kent missing but also the General's car and the General's cook. The car was subsequently found abandoned about two miles outside Queenstown, which made it obvious that the couple, who were never heard of again, had eloped to America! Thus did the Brigadier General, all in one day, lose his car, his chauffeur and his cook!

* * * * *

Early in 1908 the Battalion moved to the South Camp in Aldershot, where it became part of the 6th Infantry Brigade under Brigadier-General Colin Mackenzie. R.J.K. had given up the Adjutancy after three years in the appointment, and had taken over a Company. Just after the move he was selected as a member of the Committee of the Army Football Association; in the following October he became a member of the Selection Committee and of the Supreme Committee of the Aldershot Command Football Association.

The Battalion had come from Dublin with a good record – not only as a smart unit but as one which excelled in those sports and games which were then indulged in. The officers, many of whom were first-class athletes, boxers, etc., were an enthusiastic crowd and the most fanatical of them was R.J.K., who was in charge of football. It fell to his lot to find the grounds on which to play the various Regimental and Company competitions then in progress. All that was available was, in fact, the 6th Infantry Brigade ground which, being shared by three other Battalions, meant that the Faughs had the use of it for only six days in the month, a situation common to all other units in the Command. My uncle, therefore, made a rough survey of all the rough ground in the Barrack areas – Aldershot was still very much of a bracken and pine-tree sort of place – to see if there was not room for each unit to have its own ground at least and possibly more.

He had also noticed that Aldershot town, especially on pay nights, was a rowdy place and that it was not always safe for people to be out in the streets after nightfall. To help the civil police, strong picquets from each unit were on patrol until the public houses were closed. From his observations, and from his talk with others, he realized that the men, having nothing to do in the afternoons, took to slumbering, the prevailing practice being 'old soldiers to bed, recruits on square'. Later in the day, after tea, they would break the monotony of this existence by going off into the town to drink, look for women – and, if necessary, fight. He came to the conclusion that, although these conditions in the barracks were not entirely responsible for the drinking that went on outside, they played a potent part in bringing it about, much to the great detriment of the men's morale and health.

He discovered further that no action of any kind had been taken – or was ever contemplated – to give the troops any more recreation facilities than had existed in 1883, since which time the garrison had trebled in numbers. He conceived the idea that, if the men – no longer the old soldier type recruited for life but young short-service men – were able to work off their surplus energy instead of spending their afternoons in bed, they would be too tired to go out in the evenings. In the course of time they could be put on their honour to behave so that the town picquets, disliked by everyone concerned, could eventually be abolished.

This conception was bold and revolutionary – but what chance had a young Captain, backed though he was by his brother officers, of influencing the High Command, most of whose members had started their careers prior to the Cardwell Reforms of 1881, when the customs and traditions of the Peninsular War were still firmly entrenched? Full of hope, he put his ideas down in the form of a 'frank' memorandum and awaited his chance. It was not long in coming. Before he left the Command in 1911, not only had the picquets been abolished but there were 16 first-class football grounds and several cricket pitches in the North and South Camps alone, a figure which had risen to 114 by 1946 (See Appendix 1). In 1914 similar construction work had started in the Southern and Northern Commands under R.J.K.'s supervision (as an extra-mural activity) – and after the First World War he extended the scheme, under the aegis of the newly-formed Army Sports Control Board, to all garrisons in this country and overseas.

* * * * *

It will be agreed by those who knew him well that R.J.K. was not particularly ambitious or self-seeking for himself. A better description, perhaps, would be that he was enthusiastic and dedicated. He was never in a position to give his name to a movement because of high social rank, nor to seek honours, advancement or recognition by placing donations in the right quarters. What acknowledgement or rewards might have come his way during his lifetime usually failed to materialize because he had almost invariably upset, by some impulsive action, those who had the power to give.

In later years, though, he was upset by the way in which other people took the credit and received reward for ideas which had been his own. He was aggrieved, for instance – and the same thing applied to his second baby, the National Playing Fields Association, born in 1924 – that, in various biographies and books, General Sir Horace Smith-Dorrien was stated to be responsible for the abolition of the town picquets and for the building of the recreation grounds. It is, of course, impossible to contest such statements. A military commander, having listened to the advice of his staff and subordinates, must eventually reach a decision, the responsibility for which is his and his alone. It can equally be emphasized, on the other hand, that my uncle originated the plan, which, by his determination and drive, coupled with a modicum of youthful audacity, obtained the authority of Smith-Dorrien for its inception. It must also be recorded that he had the backing of all the higher commanders concerned, from the Brigadier-General upwards, once the scheme had been approved and activated.

6

The Idea Takes Shape

R.J.K. wrote:

Some few weeks after our arrival in Aldershot I was the guest of our Brigade Commander, Colin Mackenzie, at a small dinner party. On inquiring how we were settling down I replied that so far as the officers were concerned we were liking the place very much, having as we had, every amenity in the way of sport, e.g., hunting, polo, shooting, golf, tennis, etc., and all the facilities offered us by the Officers' Club. But as far as the men were concerned I gave the General a very different answer, and, after describing the situation, expressed surprise that successive Commanders-in-Chief at Aldershot should have come and gone without making any addition whatsoever to the handful of grounds existing for the men. The General seemed very impressed, and when I told him I had written a report on the whole situation and outlined a scheme which, in three to four years, would provide all that was required, he asked me to forward my Paper through my Commanding Officer. After reading it he sent it to the GOC, 2nd Division, and it eventually reached the GOC-in-C.

Sir Horace Smith-Dorrien sent for me to Command HQ where he expressed the same surprise and concern as Brigadier-General Colin Mackenzie had done. After a long discussion he decided to convene a conference. This was eventually attended by the Major-General i/c Administration, H.M. Lawson, both the Divisional Commanders with their senior staff officers, the Chief Engineer, the Chief Ordnance Officer, the CRE (Lands) with his Chief Clerk, Mr. Lambert – and myself. In his opening statement Sir Horace explained the circumstances, and said further that, having gone into my scheme very fully with the MGA, had decided that it should be set in motion at once and continued until finished.

So it was that on October 1, 1908, the Scheme began; all obstacles and difficulties as they arose being energetically dealt with by the committee, of which, by order of Sir Horace, I was appointed Chairman. The plan was that a permanent party of 500 men – and a further 2,000 men on route marching days – should be employed in levelling the ground; an operation which eventually assumed vast proportions, entailing, as it did, the clearance of big areas of trees, much excavation and levelling, and the deviation of existing roads, water courses and telegraph poles. All this was carried out with the help of the CRE (Lands Branch) and the Field Companies, RE.

With this organization, and above all with Sir Horace himself and his MGA both taking the greatest interest – a fact of which every senior officer was well aware – the work progressed until, within two to three years, the first batch of grounds came into play. From then onwards it was more or less plain sailing as far as the Aldershot Command was concerned, more grounds being added each year right up to the outbreak of the 1914 War.

I should here tell of a matter of importance that arose in 1913 (by which time I had been out of the Aldershot Command for nearly two years), for it tells how the Scheme came to be extended to embrace every other Command both at home and overseas.

After some Battalions or other units had been digging for two to three years they had found, on changing station, exactly the same conditions which prevailed at Aldershot in 1908. I received a number of letters from officers asking why the Scheme could not be started in all the other Commands. Armed with a letter of introduction, therefore, from Major-General H.M. Lawson, I wrote to the Permanent Under-Secretary of State for War, and at a subsequent interview with him I exposed the whole situation, urging that a general plan be prepared to cover all Commands, in which work should start simultaneously. This plan was subsequently sanctioned by the Army Council, together with the necessary injunctions to the General Officers Commanding-in-Chief.

At this time, 1913, I was Brigade Major, 6th (London) Infantry Brigade which formed part of the 2nd Division, a Territorial formation. Foregoing my winter's leave I decided to make a survey of the Southern Command first of all, since this Command not only contained the largest number of troops but was now under Sir

Horace Smith-Dorrien who, knowing me well from the Aldershot days, would give me his co-operation and help. My first visit was to Southern Command Headquarters where, in Sir Horace's absence, I saw the MGA. From there I went on to Tidworth where I made a survey of the whole Camp. After this, but on another occasion, I made a similar survey at Plymouth. Work had only just started on the digging and levelling here when the First World War broke out, the troops then having to go and dig elsewhere.

Before jumping ahead in time to 1919 in order to complete my uncle's picture of the Scheme in so far as he was personally connected with it, his separate account of the Plymouth visit is included here as an interlude of light relief from the heavy digging and excavation which was now going on day by day in all the Home Garrisons.

At the time of my visit to Plymouth troops had already started work at Tidworth where they had made considerable headway. On arrival in the city I booked a room at the Grand Hotel on the famous Hoe. Here I met Brigadier-General Beauchamp Doran, commanding 7th Infantry Brigade, who, with his wife, lived in the Hotel itself.

'Tomorrow.' he said, after we had finished dinner, 'I want you to come to Brigade HQ at Devonport to meet Major St. Leger who is President of the Garrison Sports Committee. You and he can go through the Recreation File together; then we'll all go out to have a look at the proposed sites for the ground. How will that suit you?'

'That will be excellent, Sir,' I said.

The next morning he took me to Raglan Barracks, where St. Leger (2IC of the Royal Irish Regiment) was awaiting me. Handing me the file he said, 'There you are, Kentish, go through it with St. Leger while I look through my morning's correspondence – you'll find everything in it that you want to know.' And indeed I did – as well as some things that I did not want, or was not supposed to know, for among the papers were two letters from the MGA, General Altham, which read as follows:-

January 2, 1913
'There's a young officer by the name of Kentish going round in connection with the men's recreation ground. This is to warn you to "beware of Kentish", for he made an unholy mess of Tidworth.

He not only presumes to be an expert on lay-out but construction and engineering work too. As a matter of fact he is neither. He only comes in an advisory capacity and has no executive powers whatsoever.'

and

March 20, 1913
'In continuation of the letter I wrote you about Kentish, I again want to warn you that he comes to Plymouth in an advisory capacity only. Any suggestions he puts forwards must be sent here for approval. He made an unholy mess of Tidworth and will do the same in Plymouth unless we take steps to prevent it. He came to Tidworth before I took over here, and my predecessor, thinking he was an expert, sanctioned his proposals with the results as stated.'

Both were DO letters (demi-official) and should never have been put into the file.

'Well, that's a good start,' I said to St. Leger. 'Do I give the file back to General Doran and say nothing about the letters – or what?' 'Oh, no,' replied St. Leger, 'he's got a good sense of humour and will be rather amused.' The General, half-laughing and half serious, reproved the Brigade Major for having allowed the letters to get into the file, and then said, 'As a matter of fact, I'm lunching with the C-in-C and General Altham tomorrow, so I'll have a word about you.'

The next evening Doran returned from his meeting in excellent humour and said: 'I've put matters right for you. I spoke to Sir Horace Smith-Dorrien* after lunch and, on hearing you were here, he said immediately: "Oh! Capital! He did wonders at Aldershot. You couldn't have a better man. Don't you agree, Altham?" And Altham had to say, "Yes, Sir, I do." So that is the last I think you'll hear of the unholy mess at Tidworth!'

In fairness to General Altham it should be said that the subsoil at Tidworth is chalk. When he took over as MGA there were immense heaps of this excavated soil lying about, and until these had been removed and the ground levelled and covered with turf or black soil, Tidworth did, in fact, give the appearance of a mess that was 'unholy', to say the least of it!

---

* General Sir Horace Smith-Dorrien was now GOC-in-C, Southern Command.

Before reverting to 1908 to resume my uncle's memoirs in a more chronological form, his account of the Garrison Recreation Scheme is concluded here, so as to give a complete picture of the undertaking, which from 1920 onwards, so revolutionized the soldier's outlook:

> Sometime in 1919, when commanding the Base Camp in Antwerp, I received a letter from General Sir Charles Harington, then Deputy CIGS, to inform me that he had arranged for my relief so that I could resume work on my scheme, which had come to an abrupt end in 1914. To assist me in my work, and to ensure the co-operation of the different Commands, he told me he had called a conference for all the Command Engineers, at which he wanted me to take the chair, so that I could explain what had happened up to 1914 and advise on further progress.
>
> The conference was duly held and the Chief Engineers returned to their Commands to give effect to the decisions reached. At this point I should say that two well-known firms of contractors were called in to assist generally: Messrs. Humphrey of Knightsbridge and Frank Harris Bros. of Guildford. These two firms took in hand the modernizing of what was known in those days as the 'Aldershot Command Ground', and the construction of the Rushmoor Arena, first intended for the Command Horse Show and afterwards used for the Aldershot Tattoo. Their activities also extended to Tidworth and Catterick.
>
> And so the Scheme progressed until there was hardly a garrison without its playing field. Meanwhile enquiries had come in from overseas asking for advice. I remember especially a letter from India stating it was proposed to form an Indian Army Sports Control Board. When I retired in 1924 to launch the National Playing Fields Association I left it to Col. B.C. Hartley, the Secretary of the ASCB, to carry on that part of the Scheme which remained to be completed.

In the early 1930s, whilst visiting various garrisons to ask, out of interest, how things were going, R.J.K. noticed that the grounds were often called after the name of the Formation Commanders who had been initially responsible for their construction. Although, for instance, General Sir Brian Horrocks could write to him, 'You are one of the lucky ones because you have something to show for your work; very few Generals can say this', he felt, nevertheless, that there was nothing, in fact, by which people *could* remember him. After a good deal of lobbying in influential circles at odd times, it was not until 1949 that he received a letter to inform him that the Army Council had decided to rename the Command Central Ground in Aldershot 'The Kentish Stadium'. Something, however, went wrong, so that my uncle's hope was never fulfilled, for the ground was eventually given the name of 'Harington'. But after his death, in 1956, a plaque was placed in front of the grandstand commemorating 'his services to the Army Football Association and his work in providing recreation grounds for the soldier'. This was unveiled on 29 March, 1957, by Field-Marshal Sir Gerald Templer, then the Chief of the Imperial General Staff and Colonel of the Royal Irish Fusiliers, in the presence of relatives, members of the Regiment and representatives of the ASCB.

* * * * *

The story must now hark back to the arrival of the 1st Battalion in Aldershot from Dublin in 1908. As has already been described, it had a first-class band, superb drill and discipline, and, moreover, was held in awe for its success in all forms of 'manly' sports, such as cross-country running, bayonet fencing and football – a reputation which it continued to enhance during its four years in the Command. Although, perhaps, the Battalion was never to gain much advantage from its part in the general digging operations previously described, its football team, under the energetic supervision of R.J.K – a useful player himself – rose to new heights until, in the season 1909–10, it reached the semi-final of the Army Football Cup. The match against the holders, The Royal Irish Rifles, was to be played in London on the ground of Chelsea Football Club at Stamford Bridge.

Two years before, R.J.K. had advocated the withdrawal of the picquets from Aldershot Town after dark, and the placing of soldiers on their honour to behave. They were, in fact, dispensed with in 1910, by order of Sir Horace Smith-Dorrien after the mass invasion of London by 600 Irishmen; and it will be nice to believe that this special outing was the incident which set the seal to

46

earlier deliberations on the subject.

Writing in 1943, R.J.K. gave the following description of the match in London:

In spite of the fears of the Colonel, W.H.P. Plumer, leave was given for a special train to be ordered to take the Battalion to London to see the match. 'Win or lose,' he said, with considerable trepidation, 'they'll paint the place red and we shall leave half of them behind in the guardroom at Wellington Barracks.' On the other hand, they were just as likely to paint Aldershot red if they were not allowed to go – so thus it was that hundreds of young Irishmen entrained at Aldershot for what was to be a memorable, as well as glorious, day.

Arriving at Waterloo, the buses went off over the river into the City, working their way finally towards Chelsea after a moment's stop opposite the Chelsea Palace Theatre, so that the men could be told where to go after the match. After a meal at Stamford Bridge there followed the match, which we won, after a hard game, 2–1. The men went mad with joy, but their bearing and behaviour were perfectly correct. After an excellent tea they went off to have a look round, and when we arrived at the Chelsea Palace two hours later we found 600 young soldiers, all waiting for the curtain to go up, with not a sign of drink on one of them! The show was first-class and, before the end, a message was flashed onto a screen: 'The Management thanks the Royal Irish Fusiliers for their patronage tonight and wishes them a great victory in the final.'

Everything had gone off beyond our wildest expectations. Most elated of all, however, was the Colonel, who, during the train journey home, marvelled greatly at the success of the outing. It was not until midnight, on Aldershot platform, that there occurred the first untoward incident of the day. I was walking with the Colonel when, suddenly, there was a cry of 'Up the Faughs!' from behind us. Then, one of the men, obviously drunk, rushed past us, slipped at the top of the subway steps and turned head over heels to the bottom, where he lay flat on his back.

'Damn the fellow,' said the Colonel, 'I hope he's broke his blankety neck' – but, on closer inspection, he added: 'Well, I'm damned if it isn't my servant!' Thus it was that the only man who did not play the game on that day was the Colonel's servant – and, tell it not to the men over the border, he was a Scot, by name of McNab, and he hailed from Glasgow!

47

Curious to know how 600 young Irishmen would return from their excursions yet, at the same time, fearing trouble, the authorities had furtively posted Military Foot Police behind trees on the route back to the barracks. Next day Sgt. Gardham reported to the Assistant Provost Marshal as follows: '... The Battalion fell in outside the station under the RSM and marched back to barracks. There was no case of drunkenness or disorderly conduct to report.' The C-in-C, Smith-Dorrien, sent his best congratulations to Col. Plumer, together with additional information that Sgt. Gardham's report was to be 'brought to the notice of every unit in the Command.'

This, of course, was a very kindly and well-intentioned act, but it did us a lot of harm. If there is one thing a Regiment dislikes it is having the merits of another one rammed down its throat. Having done well at football, having won the Army Cross-Country and Bayonet-Fighting Championships as well as the Duke of Connaught's Obstacle Race (three years running and in record time), this was the end of our popularity in the Command. This fact was proved conclusively a little later when, on Easter Monday, 1910, we played the Royal Marine Light Infantry in the final round at Aldershot, in front of 20,000 spectators and the Prince and Princess of Wales (soon to become King George and Queen Mary). The majority of the crowd should have been cheering us to win – for the Marines really belonged to the Royal Navy – but, on the contrary, it was just a question of seeing the Irish Fusiliers beaten. Cheering wildly for our opponents the spectators had their reward, for we were beaten in a magnificent game by two goals to nil.

Shortly afterwards, the Battalion left Aldershot for Bordon to join the 3rd Infantry Brigade. We had practically swept the board in everything after four very, very strenuous years keeping the flag flying. Although we were still in the same Command we left Aldershot with a record which has never since been beaten, and which I do not think ever *will* be!

7

The Lights go out in Europe

In February 1910, my uncle was appointed ADC to Major-General H.M. Lawson, now GOC 2nd Division at Aldershot. In this capacity he was able to carry on the good work with the sports grounds which he had initiated two years earlier. During his time as an ADC, at Christmas 1910 to be exact, he first emerges as a leg-puller in his story entitled 'A General, an old Soldier and a Turkey'. This pastime was typical of the rather rumbustious and slightly vulgar Edwardian era, which was now passing with the advent of King George V to the throne. The tone had been set by the Monarch himself, who was not averse to filling the evening trousers of a guest with sticky sweets or squirting water from a bicycle pump from behind a pillar. R.J.K's leg-pulling was neither subtle nor discreet, but basic and fundamental in its scope. He later wrote:

Shortly before Christmas, 1910, General Lawson was due to make an administrative inspection of the 2nd Hampshires, then quartered at Badajos Barracks in South Camp. A few days earlier, I happened to be having a drink in their Mess before lunch, and everything was beginning to get 'Christmassy'. Conversation turned to the approaching inspection, and a young officer, Jackie Le Hunte, temporarily commanding his Company and very anxious to put up a good show asked me if my General had any particular 'fads'.

'I don't think so,' I said. 'He likes to see the men smartly turned out and steady on parade – the usual things, you know. Oh, now I remember it. He is very keen on soldiers having large families; his

49

idea being that their sons make the best soldiers. So to encourage them he gives a turkey, on his Christmas inspections, to the man who has the biggest family in the unit. He likes the man to fall in by himself on the left flank of his Company so that he can congratulate him as he goes round!'

I thought everyone knew I was joking. But Jackie Le Hunte didn't, for immediately after lunch he went off to his Colour Sergeant to tell him all about it. 'Well, Sir,' said the Colour Sergeant, 'that's easy money for us because Pte. Long has 11 with another on the way. No one else has more than eight or nine at the most.' And, on being sent for, Pte. Long announced proudly that Mrs. Long had just 'obliged' again. So the turkey was certainly in the bag for 'C' Company, and Pte. Long's Christmas dinner was assured!

When the great day came, there were the gallant Hampshires all drawn up waiting for the General to arrive; and there was the equally gallant Pte. Long standing all by himself on the left flank of his Company, his chest stuck out not one, but nearly two miles! Then came the General, and the inspection commenced.

After walking down the ranks of 'A' and 'B' Companies, he came to 'C' Company where he was received by Le Hunte. Down the ranks he went with Jackie on one side of him and the Colonel on the other. On reaching the left of the front rank he came across Pte. Long standing all by himself.

'What's that man doing there?' he asked.

'Pte. Long, Sir,' said Le Hunte, 'winner of your turkey. He has 12 children, sir!'

'What on earth is he talking about?' muttered the General, and, after making some incomprehensible noises in his throat, passed on to the rear rank, leaving Pte. Long the most disappointed man on earth and Le Hunte completely bewildered.

When the whole story came out, as it did after the General's departure, the whole Battalion laughed long and loud at Jackie Le Hunte but, nevertheless, there was a note of sympathy for Pte. Long and his Christmas dinner. When the General and I were lunching afterwards, he told me about this extraordinary man and his turkey. Naturally I had to apologize, offering at the same time, to see that he got it. But the General, who had a great sense of humour, not only bought the bird himself but actually took it round personally to the Longs, much to their delight.

Ending his days as an ADC on 31 March, 1911, R.J.K. returned to the 1st Battalion, now in Bordon and under the command of Lt-Colonel D.W. Churcher. This was shortly after the centenary of the Battle of Barrosa. About this time, too, a reinforcement arrived in the shape of a Second Lieutenant from the Cavan Militia; the very same, in fact, who ten years earlier had attended Andy Dunn's military band concerts in Belfast. Passing, one day, a squad of men resting on a bank, he acknowledged their rising to attention by a negligent wave of his cane which betokened his belief that all things were his. A call from an unseen officer, however, brought him swiftly to earth, when he came face to face with R.J.K., who, speaking in a kindly tone, pointed out that these men had paid him the compliment of rising, and that the least return would be to acknowledge their gesture by a more courteous sign of appreciation. This was an early lesson, and one which was not forgotten by the man from Cavan!

In June 1911 the Battalion moved to Shorncliffe, and in February 1913 my uncle was appointed Brigade Major, 6th (London) Infantry Brigade, a Territorial formation in the London District. As this date coincided more or less with the extension of the playing ground scheme to Commands other than Aldershot, it would be convenient to surmise that this appointment was nothing more than a sinecure to enable him to devote a considerable portion of his time to travelling round the countryside, to supervize the laying of new grounds.

* * * * *

War with Germany broke out in August 1914. Amidst scenes of wild enthusiasm and fervour the BEF crossed over to France and Belgium; with it went the 1st Battalion as part of the 10th Infantry Brigade, under Brigadier-General J.A.L. Haldane, in the 4th Division. On arrival, the Division formed the newly constituted III Corps commanded by Major-General W.P. Pulteney. My uncle remained sulkily, perforce, at home as a Brigade Major in the 2nd London Division. After several unsuccessful attempts to be relieved of his appointment, he duly turned up, however, in the 1st Battalion lines where, a few days later, he was to win one of the earliest DSOs of the War at Houplines. It could never be confirmed how he came to evade authority. It was freely believed, though, that, having smuggled himself on to a boat at Southampton, he had eventually got to the correct place by a series of sojourns in train lavatories and journeys on the hoof. To those who knew him at the time, this version of his escape was quite credible; yet, as one of his contemporaries has sadly observed, of little interest to the present generation, which neither knows nor cares for the stuff of heroes.

At this juncture the Battalion, having taken part with the 4th Division in the Retreat from Mons and the Battles of Le Cateau, Marne and Aisne, was now back on the Belgian frontier, poised to attack Armentières, which it duly captured. On 17 October, the 10th Infantry Brigade, with the Faughs leading, had passed successfully through the suburb of Houplines. But on the road leading north-eastward to Frélinghien there was an unwarranted delay, caused by four isolated, though determined, Saxons who, apparently under the impression that the British cut the throats of their prisoners, were strongly holding out in a farmhouse – known locally as Phillipeaux, but to ourselves as Sydney Street Farm. The leading platoon having been held up, the remainder of the advanced guard came to its aid – with similar results. The company commander, Captain Miles Carbery, was mortally wounded, and several men had just lost their lives in a gallant attempt to fire at close quarters whilst the wounded were extricated from view. Unfortunately no artillery had been allotted on this day, so no efforts could be made to blow the building down.

At 4 p.m. the Brigade Commander, J.A.L. Haldane, rode up from Armentières to view the scene. Having ordered the farmhouse to be set on fire – which was done with great danger with our wounded lying in the vicinity – and having also suggested it should be blown down with an RE's charge, he retired back to town where he was entertained by the Mayor. Later in the evening a French liaison officer, Lt. Corblet, came to report that his efforts at 'parleying' with the Saxons had only been answered by a bullet which grazed his cheek! In the absence of any explosives, the Brigadier went off to H.Q. 5th Division to borrow an 18-pounder gun – but this did not arrive until after 11 p.m.

Once again he returned to view the now burning farm. Here he was met by R.J.K., who told him he had obtained an explosive which was nearly ready to be blown. The two of them took shelter until a loud explosion took place. Running forward, they were able to witness the end of this irritating affair which had cost so much time and so many lives.

For his gallantry in trying to rescue the wounded from the burning debris and for his initiative in obtaining the explosive, R.J.K. was awarded the DSO, Lt. Corblet an MC, and several Fusiliers the DCM. Of the wounded who were trapped in the open, my uncle wrote:

> I had occasion to lead a party to the rescue of some men on whom red hot tiles were falling. We got them all out, one by one, but left behind Pte. Kelly, one of the rescue party. Although lying wounded within a few feet of the door behind which the Germans were firing, he raised himself slowly on his hands, and with a smile on his face cried out: 'Bravo, the Faughs. We've got 'em all out, anyhow.' Then, with a huge gaping wound in his groin, he fell forward and died. I can see the smile on his face now and shall never forget it. A brave man if ever there was one.

My uncle was supposed to have been recommended for the Victoria Cross. Whether fact or fiction, the idea was certainly in the minds of the higher Commanders. On 2 December, the decorations were presented at Nieppe by the King who, that night or the night before, was staying with General Douglas Haig. The latter recorded in his diary a conversation with his guest on the subject of VCs for those who rescued wounded comrades under fire. The King thought that it should be awarded for such an action, but Haig replied that under certain circumstances, such as entering a burning building, it might well be given, although not, naturally, on every occasion.

Less than 1000 yards from Sydney Street Farm the advance petered out, both sides occupying a trench system which was still in use four years later. Half way through November the 4th Division moved a few miles northwards to the Nieppe-Ploegstreert area, where the Faughs took up their position in a flooded marshy piece of country, with the River Douvre between themselves and the Germans, who were now sitting on the Messines ridge, recently captured in their offensive against our salient to the east of Ypres. For the next five months the Battalion and the 1st battalion, Seaforth Highlanders relieved each other with monotonous regularity, on a basis of four days in and four out.

This was a comparatively easy sector of the front; quiet because the floods did not encourage the Germans to leave their newly won ridge, yet unpleasant because the winter was excessively hard and our supply of shells was, at this juncture, abysmally low. No one had envisaged or planned for a war lasting more than a few weeks; much less had anyone dreamt that Kitchener would suddenly raise 70 new divisions!

October 1914 to April 1915 saw the beginning of trench warfare in earnest, with both sides leaning all there was to know about it. This was almost the first time for many centuries that it was considered uncowardly to take cover. The gentleman's wars had gone for ever. The Douve Sector, in particular, has been immortalized by Bruce Bairnsfather, an officer in the Warwickshire Regiment in the same Brigade, in his book *Bullets and Billets*. As Battalion MGO he describes his life: four days 'out', then four days 'in', wandering nocturnally on visits to his gun sites over soggy turnip fields interspersed with three-sided farmhouses with a rectangle of smell in the middle! And, being an artist, he soon started to draw his famous Bairnsfather pictures of 'Ole Bill, Bert and Alf. Jokes, he remarked, seemed to stick out of all the horrible discomfort. The humour emitted by his phlegmatic soldiers, clad in balaclava helmets and sheepskin coats and standing in their flooded trenches, show a cheerfulness which it would be hard to beat.

That was probably the long and short of it: how best to keep the troops cheerful under such dreary conditions for six months at a stretch. At this game my uncle was particularly efficient, being as he was, quite oblivious to rebuffs from above in his efforts to get the very best for his men, to save them from the inconveniences of thoughtless orders or to cut right through red tape.

One of his efforts in December 1914 is worthy of note. A gourmand and a gourmet – he liked everything to be just so – he saw no reason why the best should not be available even in flooded trenches. With the help of Fortnum and Mason hampers, reinforced by a daily bottle of champagne – which came up for him mysteriously from the back areas – and aided or abetted by his cook, Pte. Atter, he had established quite a notable Company Mess. The meal he gave one night to two visitors was memorable enough to be included in the autobiography of the late Lady Londonderry – but it also got him into trouble. His description follows:

A few days before I had an invitation from Castlereagh, an old friend from Sandhurst days, to dine at Corps HQ where he was ADC to General Pulteney. I accepted with pleasure, for I not only knew I should dine well but I was also invited to have a bath, a luxury of the first order in those days.

And so, on the day appointed, I went off to the Chateau, where I was received '*en prince*'; and, after a marvellous bath, sat down to an excellent dinner cooked by their French chef, a refugee from Lille. All good things must come to an end, and so did this dinner. As I was leaving I asked Castlereagh to come and dine with me when we were back in the line, adding, 'What about next Tuesday? Bring any one else you like, but we can't manage more than two.'

Next morning I sent for our two faithful henchmen. Atter and Rushmore, told them about the guests and left it to them to prepare a menu. Within an hour they returned and laid one before me good enough for anyone.

On the following Tuesday, Castlereagh arrived after dark, bringing with him Brigadier General 'Tavish' Davidson (then Chief of Staff at Corps HQ and later to be Director of Military Operations to Haig at GHQ). Greetings over, we sat down to dinner – exactly as it had been planned by Atter and Rushmore – in the cellar of a moated farmhouse a few yards from the German trenches. After the meal was over I took my guests round the line to show them the kind of life the men were actually leading, for trench warfare was an innovation and the Staff had little idea of the appalling conditions under which we lived. When we got back to the cellar Tavish Davidson, who combined a rare knowledge of Staff and Regimental duties all in one, asked if there was anything he could do for us on return to Corps HQ. 'Yes', I said, 'what the men want very badly is a double issue of rum and tea. They are up to their hocks in mud and water; it would be a Godsend to them – and another thing, it's useless sending fresh meat up, they can't cook it.' 'Right,' said Tavish – and together the two of them left the Moated Farm for their 'comfy' Chateau.

A day or so later, when O'Gorman, my CQMS, arrived up after nightfall he brought news of a double issue of tea and rum – and 'tinned meat, sor, there's to be no more fresh meat in the trenches. But I'm almost forgetting it, there's a letter from Battalion HQ for you.' And he handed me a foolscap size envelope with 'Confidential' written across it.

The telephone wires had been humming between Division and Brigade, between Brigade and Battalion. 'Please explain why Capt. Kentish complained direct to Corps HQ that the rations were inadequate. His reasons for this irregular conduct are called for, etc. etc.' Correspondence floated backwards and forwards for several days. My uncle finally wrote, 'If the Brigade Commander had bothered to visit me in the same way – which he never has – I should have put in the same request. Vive le red tape!' This explanation was not, he thought, passed back by the CO, Lt.-Col. Arnold Burrowes, as no more was heard on the subject. It was the first, but by no means last, occasion when he was going to use what he called 'Friends at Court' to get what he wanted.

It was about this time, December 1914, that R.J.K., wearing his 'double-breasted blue lambskin-lined reefer coat and an old scarlet bobsleigh cap with a tassel on it – just like the brewers' men wore – and carrying a big shepherd's crook stick' was accosted by a soldier, who said, 'Ye've got to go on leave, sor! There's a car waitin' for yer behind the church in Plugstreet.' Hurriedly handing over the Company, he called out to the men, 'What shall I bring you fellows back?'

'A gramophone, sor,' said one. 'A drum and a couple of flutes,' called another – and a third suggested 'Kippers'. A week later he was back with the lot, including a barrel of kippers. 'And the next morning there was a great cooking of kippers and best of all, the wind was blowing in the direction of the German trenches so that they got full benefit of the smell, much to the delight of everyone in the Company.' This peculiar man, who could discuss the merits of a Bordelaise or a Bearnaise sauce with a top-notch chef, had also a curious appetite for the humbler types of fish, which seemed to tickle his sense of humour as well as his palate.

On 18 December, R.J.K. was promoted Major. On Christmas Eve, just before the Battalion was due for relief, some Saxons, who had been singing carols in the trenches opposite, made overtures for a temporary truce. Gerald Hill and other kindred spirits went to investigate, after which there was a general swapping of cigarettes and photographs. When the Battalion returned on 28 December the truce was still on, but, on 31 December, the Saxons warned that they were due for relief by Bavarians, for whose attitude they could not answer. The Germans tried this again in subsequent years at various places. It was sternly forbidden by the powers that were, and, in 1916, two officers in the Brigade of Guards were court-martialled, one being acquitted.

Life went monotonously on until mid-April 1915, when the Germans launched an all-out offensive against our salient to the east of Ypres, breaking the line in several places with the help of a new ally, chlorine gas. The 3rd Division was rushed into the salient to take part in the heavy fighting, which was to last, with very heavy casualties, until mid-May. The brunt of the attack had been borne by the Second Army, whose Commander, Sir Horace Smith-Dorrien, had shortened his line accordingly, much to the annoyance of the French Army on his left. It was decided that this man, who had fought (and won) the Battle of Le Cateau against orders to the contrary, should be replaced. The Commander-in-Chief, Sir John French, feeling unable to deliver the coup-de-grace personally, sent across his Chief of Staff, General 'Wully' Robertson (later to be CIGS at the War Office) to do the dirty work. It was on this occasion that Robertson, the only private soldier to have carried a baton in his knapsack, made the famous remark, ''Orace, yer fer 'ome.'

8

Lancs, Balls and Pork

In the middle of May 1915, R.J.K. was put in temporary command of the 1st Battalion, The East Lancashire Regiment, a unit in the 4th Division, which had suffered crippling casualties. Here he remained until 24 September. He had his own ideas and his own methods, which were undoubtedly successful, as to how a Battalion should be run. By his seniors he was considered an appalling nuisance, and by the more conservative members of GHQ as an Antichrist. In a short time, however, he had brought the East Lancashires to a high state of efficiency with an injection of his personality, this being the secret of his success.

One evening he was sitting in his HQ – the Battalion was in the line at the time – when in walked Major General Louis Bols, Chief of Staff at 3rd Army HQ, accompanied by his GSO2, Major Blunt. 'We've just had a look round the front line,' said the visitor, with a twinkle in his eye, 'and by the way, I wish you'd let your people know that I spell my name with an "o" and one "l", and not an "a" and two "l"s.' Then, after exchanging pleasantries, the two disappeared into the darkness .

Next day an inquiry was made on the phone to Major Blunt as to the meaning of the General's remarks, from whom R.J.K. learnt that when they were approaching Battalion HQ in the dark the following conversation had taken place with a sentry:

' 'Alt! Who goes there?'

'General Bols and Staff Officer.'

'Who are yer? What's yer name?'

'I'm General Bols.'

'To 'ell with yer bloody balls. What's yer name?'

'Bols – B-O-L-S.'

'Advance, Balls, and let's 'ave a look at yer, lad.' After an inspection at close quarters the satisfied sentry said, 'Pass, Sir, all's well.'

'Thanks,' replied R.J.K., 'but if a General must have a name like that, what can he expect?'

Someone else with a dubious name in the vicinity was Lt.-Col. the Hon. Charles Palk (pronounced Pork), commanding 1st Battalion The Hampshire Regiment. A gallant officer, but rather pompous and eccentric, he had violent dislikes, including the 1st Battalion, the East Lancashire Regiment, which he always referred to as the 'East Lancs'. My uncle had occasion to write to Charles Palk – they were in the same Brigade – and he asked a clerk to put it in an envelope and see that it was delivered. Sometime later a letter arrived marked 'Private and Confidential'.

'Don't you think it about time that your bloody East Lancs knew how to spell my name. I might be just a "piece of pork" for all anyone cares. And there is no such Regiment as the 1st Hants, but there is a 1st Battalion, The Hampshire Regiment.' The offending envelope, which was enclosed with the letter, had been addressed to: Lt.-Col. the Hon. Charles Pork, Comdg. The 1st Hants. This called for a reciprocal letter from R.J.K., who equally denied the existence of the 'East Lancs' – but it had no effect.

Charles Palk (pronounced Pork) was killed on the first day of the Battle of the Somme a year later, together with two other Battalion Commanders and the Brigade Commander. But my uncle was no longer with them then.

The Brigade Commander, C.B. Prowse, was a man my uncle remembered and had a great admiration for, but his HQ sent very humorous messages or so they seemed to him at the time.

Message (received two hours before an attack and after the biscuit and plum and apple jam arrived up with great difficulty): 'I want your men to have a substantial breakfast before the attack.'

Reply: 'Please send up at once 1000 steaks, 1000 new laid eggs and 1000 kippers. Will then be able to comply.'

Message: 'Mincing machines are to be issued for those men

whose teeth cannot cope with the ration biscuit. Inform number required.'

Reply: 'MO now inspecting men's teeth. When completed will inform you how many machines required for each man.'

Message: 'The river in your sector has fallen two feet in the last 24 hours. Report for information Corps Commander to what you attribute this.'

Reply: 'I attribute this to the extraordinary and certainly very abnormal thirst of the fishes in this river.'

The last reply brought Prowse hurrying down to a RV behind a certain ruined church. He seemed most upset, thought my uncle. 'Look,' he said, 'you've got to stop sending these silly answers whenever the spirit moves you. I've had both Divisional and Corps Commanders on the phone today. The latter was furious and asked, "Who is this fellow Kentish?" I explained that you were my best Commanding Officer, but he was far from convinced. These messages are mostly written by Staff learners, and you have thoroughly upset everybody.'

9

Leadership and Morale

R.J.K. commanded the 1st Battalion of his Regiment in the Somme area from September to November 1915, in which month he was appointed to start off the 3rd Army School at Flixécourt, the first of its kind and the model on which countless others were to be subsequently organized. In his history of the 1st Battalion during the Great War, Brigadier General Arnold Burrowes wrote, 'His withdrawal was a great loss to the 87th. No officer could have devoted his life more fully to the welfare of his Regiment. His very successful efforts to improve facilities for sport in the Army, especially at Aldershot, had made him one of the best known officers throughout the service, and his constant care for those under him had the inevitable result of securing their devotion to him.'

We now come to his great speciality during the First World War: leadership, morale and *esprit de corps.* By November 1918 it could be said that the BEF in Europe reigned supreme as a cohesive force capable of going forward against the enemy. The Russians had revolted, the French had mutinied in 1916 and were now incapable of a sustained offensive; the Americans, still raw, had to keep popping out of the line for a snack, owing to a breakdown of their 'transportation'. In early 1918 the Portuguese, embittered that only officers could have home leave, and that one of their commanders was running his formation from Paris – where he was immensely popular – had decided to leg it, exposing the flank, incidentally, of the Brigade which my uncle was commanding at Festubert. Taking off their boots to run the faster, they had then purloined the machines of a British cyclist battalion.

But somehow the BEF, in spite of the biggest bloodbaths of all time at the Somme, 1916 and Passchendaele in 1917, had retained its equanimity and its faith in the C-in-C, Sir Douglas Haig. In this it had received no encouragement at all from the politicians. To his son, a front-line officer, Lloyd George wrote, 'Kitchener! What a wonderful poster he made ... Haig! Brilliant to the top of his riding boots.' Haig, secretly writing in his diary, thought Lloyd George 'cunning ... shifty ... unreliable.... He seems a cur.... He appears to be a thorough impostor.' The clever upstart, Lloyd George, however, failed to displace the aristocratic Haig, who religiously believed that the war would be won in France – and nowhere else. It was left to this imperturbable, though unimaginative, commander to prove himself correct. In this he was ably assisted by the British soldier, who remained loyal and cheerful to the end.

R.J.K. strongly maintained that our success was due to good morale and *esprit de corps* caused by our local leadership at all levels. No doubt he was partly right; at least we did not command our Brigades from Paris nor confine home leave to officers only. But at the end of the summer of 1915, to go back three years, the standard of leadership was in a state of deterioration. Casualties in the regular units had been high. The newly arrived Kitchener and Territorial Divisions, for the same reason, were led by youngsters who had little idea of the history behind the badges they wore, or how to look after the men.

An officer in the 3rd Army, Capt. (later Major-General) J.F.C. Fuller, had previously written a small book, *Training Soldiers for War.* This, quite fortuitously, had got into the hands of General A.L. Lynden-Bell, Chief of Staff at 3rd Army HQ, who suggested that an Army School should be opened to aim at instructing 50 officers and 50 NCOs for a month at a time in discipline, patriotism, *esprit de corps,* etc. Fuller, then a GSO3 at HQ VII Corps, was co-opted to organize it. Having found a chateau at Flixécourt and made out the first syllabus, he then recommended my uncle as the best man in the 3rd Army to run it.

The school opened in October/November 1915, and here R.J.K was in his element. With plenty of visitors coming to see how it worked, he had ample opportunities to demonstrate his flair for showmanship. An ardent believer in the telephone, he achieved administrative perfection by badgering to death those who had something to provide. At home my father used to display a notice – quite uselessly – which read: 'This telephone is yours at will; I merely have to pay the bill', but at Flixécourt the cost was borne by HM Government, with no Big Brother to register disapproval.

The courses started off with three addresses by the Commandant on Morale, Leadership and *Esprit de Corps*. Before the war he had entered for the RUSI gold medal essay on these subjects when he had relied on the maxims – on which his future teaching was based – laid down by Lord Wolseley in his *Soldier's Pocketbook*. These maxims, together with the three initial addresses, were published by Gale and Polden, the Aldershot printers, in 1917.

The following March just after the School had left Flixécourt for Aussi-le-Chateau, near Amiens, he initiated COs Conferences for a week at a time, where 20 or 30 COs and senior officers met for discussions. At the crucial moment, however, he was promoted to command 76 Infantry Brigade in the 3rd Division with the rank of Brigadier General, which formation he was to lead during the Battle of the Somme in July. In place of the newly arrived Commandant, Major J.F.C. Fuller, now GSO2, 37th Division, stepped in to run the first Conference, which was a great success. These Conferences were continued on a higher level at Aldershot towards the end of the year, in the form of the Senior Officers School, of which my uncle was the first official Commandant, through which hundreds had to pass before being allowed to command a battalion. Starting off in October 1916, this new school embraced after a time an Instructors School to train those who were to staff the dozens of training establishments springing up like mushrooms.

Why at Aldershot? With 300 students at a time, this new venture was probably beyond the capacity of the back area of the battle zone in France. One also gets the lurking suspicion that certain elements at GHQ were only too glad to see the last of this human bomb which had pestered them for so long. If Haig wanted him to go to England, then the dugouts at home could bear the brunt of it. After the Battle of the Somme, in which he had commanded the 76th Infantry Brigade, my uncle had sent a 16-page report to HQ 4th Army, criticizing certain aspects of staff work. This had included better ways of doing things so that more success might be achieved with fewer casualties. It was a bold and risky thing to do, but he had little fear of higher authority.

In an interview with General Douglas Haig at GHQ, he had been told, 'I am sending you back to Aldershot to organize this new School because, judging from reports from my Army Commanders, I learn that Majors and Senior Captains have little knowledge of the duties of a Commanding Officer. To give them this knowledge I am sending them to you, so that when they return they will not only know how to lead their men in the attack but how to get them into the right mood to follow them.' This last, of course, was the crux of the matter: how to get soldiers to 'get up and go' into an artillery barrage or machine gun fire if they have neither affection nor a feeling of trust for the officer concerned.

'I want you to concentrate on leadership and morale and leave the tactical side to your staff,' were Haig's last instructions. It was thus a great honour for R.J.K. to be chosen for this assignment out of the 200 or so Brigadier Generals to be found at that time in France.

A great help in the teaching of leadership were the 'Maxims' of Field Marshal Viscount Wolseley, contained in his *Soldier's Pocketbook*. The publication of this, in the last quarter of the nineteenth century, had inflamed the Duke of Cambridge, Commander-in-Chief at the Horse Guards and cousin of Queen Victoria. This was still a time when the 'presence of the individual' was considered unnecessary as the machine was so perfect. The words 'Carry on, Sergeant' were, metaphorically, all that was required for a young officer to depart for a day's hunting or shooting once or twice a week – or even longer. Lord Wolseley had complained that many soldiers only knew their officers as someone who moved them about on the parade ground and kept order by a system of severe punishment. An officer should make himself loved and respected by being intimate but without loss of dignity; he should study his men's individual characters and take a lively interest in their amusements. Napoleon was, above all, a student of character and could extract from his soldiers everything they were capable of. If you want to win battles, you must have the affection of those you lead.

Thus was R.J.K. inspired in his teaching of leadership and morale. There had always been an idea that only very few men were born leaders or naturally capable of man management. That is not true, he taught. A man must develop an understanding of human nature; he must always be asking himself what he can do for his men and how he can help them. He must look after their comfort, both in the trenches and in billets behind the line; he must always be cheerful and optimistic. That must surely be within the capacity of all officers and, if practiced, they will find they have gained the respect and affection of their men, who will follow them anywhere.

* * * * *

In the autumn of 1916, therefore, R.J.K. stepped, one dark and dirty night, onto a boat at Calais. 'Out at sea,' he wrote, 'the boat gave a tremendous lurch, and into me was cannoned a young officer, who apologized. "That's all right," I replied, "going on leave?" "I was – and going to get married too – but yesterday my CO said I had to go to some bloody place at Aldershot called the Senior Officers' School." "Then you needn't worry," I said, "for I'm the bloody Commandant!" That's how I made the acquaintance of Capt. ("Sapper") McNeile, the author of the famous *Bulldog Drummond* books; and at the end of the Course I was able to keep him on as an instructor, with the rank of Lt.-Col.'

'Sapper' had one further shock to come. On the first day of the course all students were ordered to parade at 7 a.m. without having been called by the batmen first. On the parade ground, cold and miserable, they were put through their paces for an hour by the Adjutant. At 8 a.m. my uncle rode on to dismiss them with the words: 'Well, gentlemen, now you know just what your men feel like when you get them on to an early parade with no food inside them. Never let it happen! Now we'll dismiss for breakfast.'

This was their first and rather dramatic lesson in the way R.J.K thought a Battalion should be run. Besides tactics and drill they were to be taught, down to the very last detail, how to manage their subordinates; dress, discipline, recreation, leave, billets, welfare – even down to the type of food which produced indigestion or, alternatively, 'peace of mind with all men except the Hun'. The addresses given and the lessons taught were afterwards printed and published by Messrs. Gale and Polden. If nowhere else, they are at least available to posterity in the Library of the British Museum.

After the end of the courses R.J.K. travelled back to France to deliver reports on the suitability of each student to command, as well as to pick up the 'latest' from the Army HQs. The School continued as such after the War, until it was merged into the School of Infantry at Warminster.

In July 1917 the School was inspected by the King and his uncle, the Duke of Connaught. This was followed by a private dinner party in the Royal Pavilion, Aldershot, which, in addition to my uncle, was attended by Queen Mary, Prince Albert (later King George VI), and Princess Mary (later Countess of Harewood). After the ladies had withdrawn from the dinner table, there was much praise for what the school was doing, and then the King talked about a domestic social problem which was worrying him.

'I have recently had a letter from a man who was once a Sergeant in the Coldstream Guards. After leaving the Colours he became one of my lodge keepers at Sandringham. In 1914 he was recalled to the Colours, got a Commission from the ranks and eventually became a Captain. Then he was badly wounded and discharged with a wound pension and the rank of Captain. Now he is asking for his old job back again. How can I have a Captain as a lodge keeper? If I do not take him back, what will he do?'

'Most difficult, Sir,' said the Duke, 'unless he gives up his rank.'

'Why should he,' said the King, 'after being promoted for gallantry in the field.'

'A most difficult problem, Sir,' repeated the Duke.

In these more democratic days it might not be such a problem, but whether the King ever took his exalted lodge keeper back again my uncle never heard.

It was at this cosy dinner party that R.J.K. probably laid the foundation of a future friendship with the Royal Family which was going to serve him in good stead in the years to come.

10

War and Peace

After 14 months at Aldershot R.J.K. was back in France again, in command of 166 Infantry Brigade in the 55th Division. As such he was present during the last German offensive of 1918 when, in spite of having his flank exposed by the fleeing Portuguese (boot-less and on stolen bicycles!), he succeeded in holding his ground at Givenchy on La Bassée Canal, a bastion formed to defend the important town of Bethune and which formed the pivot of the German attack on the British front as far north as Merckhem by the sea in Belgium.

It was the beginning of the end when, in October 1918, the Germans started to retreat. Having advanced to the river Dendre, 166 Infantry Brigade established its HQ in the only house which was left standing in the village of Cysing, the remainder having been demolished by the retreating enemy. The Divisional Commander, Major General A.S. Jeudwine, had dropped in *en passant* and was afterwards heard to say to his staff officer, 'Kentish is a b----- fool to occupy that house; it's a sitting target for artillery fire, and I bet it has been mined.' As a matter of fact it had already been cleared by a detachment of Sappers, but Jeudwine was not to know that.

Sure enough, the Brigade HQ staff had just settled down to the evening meal when high-explosive shells started to burst all round the house – without hitting it – for a good 10 minutes. No more came, nor did any for the next two days. By the fourth day, how-ever, it would seem that the Divisional Commander was bent on scaring my uncle out of his – comparatively – comfortable house, a sitting target though it was. He and his staff had just sat down for the evening meal when a motor despatch rider from Divisional HQ arrived with a letter marked 'Confidential and Urgent'.

'In other areas houses have been blown up by delayed action mines as long as 12 days after the German retreat. The Divisional Commander wishes you to make a very careful examination of your HQ and have the floors and foundations dug up and searched for mines as a test case.'

A cheerful letter after four days have passed, thought R.J.K., and, asking for a message pad, he took the opportunity to send one of his silly answers to what he considered to be a silly message: 'Yours received in the middle of dinner. We are all about to have one more glass of port and then systematically dig up the foundations for the German mines, putting our trust in the Lord. Seems to me to be a case of four holes up and eight to play.'

But the fifth and subsequent holes of this game were never played for, on the following day, orders were received to continue the advance against the retreating Germans. And the War was to end very shortly with the signing of the Armistice in early November; thus ending four years of slaughter and wasted resources.

Two years later R.J.K., in the house of mutual friends near Konstanz, was to meet the Princess von Thurn und Taxis, an aristocratic lady in her late seventies. In the course of conversation on a subject which interested him, he was amazed to hear her say: 'You know, General, our Army was never beaten. It was the people at home who were beaten. As your blockade tightened so the German mothers in the cities and the towns, with their children crying out for food, wrote to their husbands at the front, telling about their suffering. So our soldiers put their heads together and stopped fighting.' That may have been half the truth, thought my uncle, nevertheless we had given them a tremendous pounding in the field, and he had seen them running like hares. He took her point, though: morale had cracked on the home front.

Had the fighting continued, he might well have commanded a Division. He had done well for himself. After deserting his post in England to join his Regiment in France, he had won one of the earliest DSOs of the war. Then he had commanded two Battalions and two Brigades after rising from Captain to Brigadier General in two years. But his main achievement had been to organize and command the 3rd Army School at Flixécourt, followed later by the Senior Officers School at Aldershot. The teaching of leadership and morale had been his absorbing interest; he was going to return to it in the Second World War at the age of 64, wearing the extinct uniform of a Brigadier General. A dugout, indeed! But his upward path had always been difficult owing to the contempt he felt, where necessary, for Higher Authority, feelings he never failed to express openly. He had finally got under the skin of the Commander-in-Chief Home Forces, Sir John French, during his time at Aldershot.

In 1941, during the early days of the Second World War, Sir Winston Churchill minuted the following: 'Who is the General of this Division and does he take part in the cross-country runs himself? ... in my experience officers with high athletic qualifications are not usually successful in higher ranks.' The officer in question was, of course, General Montgomery – but in R.J.K.'s case the answer will never be known, for his ability to command a Division was nipped in the bud by the ending of hostilities. Yes! Montgomery certainly took part in the cross-country runs, but he was also one of those men capable of getting men to follow him by his personal approach – the true test of good leadership and one of those things that R.J.K. took such pains to teach in the First World War. 'Monty' gained the affection of his men because they were confident that he would be economical with their lives. Again this was what my uncle had stressed in his 16-page report to 4th Army HQ, at the risk of losing his job, after the Battle of the Somme in 1916. He had a great admiration for Montgomery. In 1945 he wrote to the Under-Secretary of State for War, Brigadier General Lord Croft, who was a personal friend of his: 'Dear Henry, Haig should have been made a Duke in 1918. Montgomery (and Alexander) should be made Dukes in 1945. Don't get it wrong this time.' But 'Monty' did worse than Haig, for only a Viscountcy came his way.

* * * * *

If the British Expeditionary Force in France had kept its equilibrium during four years of fighting, it certainly lost control of itself in its stampede towards the promised land; fit for heroes, the politicians thought, but, unfortunately, lacking the milk and honey. After the Armistice in November R.J.K. was put to organizing and commanding the Base Camp at Antwerp, through which a proportion of the heroes were to pass on their way home. It was two years later that he happened to give a talk to the people of Poplar, in the East End of London, under the chairmanship of George Lansbury, the popular MP known as 'the uncrowned King of Poplar'. Afterwards the lecturer was asked to the home of the Lansburys to meet the wife and 13 children of the MP, where he was told that the people of Poplar, poor though they might be, 'were all right'. 'It's that man George,' said Lansbury, referring to Lloyd George, the Prime Minister, 'who was all wrong, and I will tell you why! If I asked George once I asked him a hundred times, both in and out of the House, that, when the War came to an end, only the skilled, the employable and those who had occupations waiting for them should be released. All the younger men who had never had time to learn a trade should be sent to workshops or schools of instruction until they became employable. Don't, I implored him, flood the market with thousands and thousands of unskilled and unemployable men all at once. But what did George do? He released three million men and is now wondering why the country is in the greatest state of unrest for the last hundred years...' 'That was partly caused,' R.J.K. reminded him, 'by the newspaper, the *Daily Herald,* producing a banner headline, "THE WAR IS OVER. SEND OUR BOYS HOME". The direct result had been that many of the military camps – and I was commanding one – broke out in open mutiny or carried out acts of insubordination which their Officers were powerless to prevent.' Mr Lansbury, no longer at that particular time editor of the *Daily Herald,* remembered this, but seemed glad to change the subject!

Life apparently had not been a bed of roses in the Base Camp at Antwerp. In 1919, however, my uncle was called back to England to command the 6th (London) Infantry Brigade and then the Surrey and Middlesex Brigade, both Territorial formations situated in central London. Thus he was able to install himself in the

Hyde Park Hotel, the first of many such establishments in which he was to live for the next 35 years. To look after him he had an ex-soldier called Hillson, who, attired in a black coat and bowler hat, acted as valet and general factotum to this incredibly active and ubiquitous individual, who was to be described by the British Olympic Association in 1924 – although no more precise qualification was given – as 'probably the greatest enthusiast in England today'.

Co-incidental with his duties as a Brigade Commander – not very onerous, one might suspect – he came under the aegis of General Sir Charles Harington, Deputy Chief of the Imperial General Staff. Sir Charles was head of the newly formed Army Sports Control Board at the (then) War Office, and he wanted R.J.K. to preside at a meeting of Command Engineers with the object of continuing the scheme for garrison playing grounds which had come to such an abrupt end in 1914. So he had the task, over the next few years, of supervising what went on, which entailed journeys as far as Fort George in Scotland, Bodmin in Cornwall and Ipswich in the Eastern Counties. Included in this programme, for which civil engineering firms were employed, was the re-structuring of the Central Stadium at Aldershot with a proper spectators' stand and fixed seating, and the building of the Rushmoor Arena, the future site of the searchlight Tattoos and Horse Shows.

The supervision of the layout of the Garrison Grounds might well have satisfied a middle-aged man, but R.J.K. had fingers in other pies as well. During the last few years of his army career he was a member of the Army Sports Control Board Council (1919–1925), Hon. Sec. Army Football Association to 1922, then Vice-President Army Fencing Union, Founder of the British Modern Pentathlon Association, Co-founder of the Boys' Army Cup Competition and Co-founder of the Triangular Football Tournament between the British, French and Belgian Armies – now known as the Kentish Cup in this Country and 'Le Kentish' abroad. To these can be added membership of the Amateur Athletic Association, the Football Association Council, Chairman of the Dockland Settlements Committee in Canning Town (an Old Malvernian Missionary activity), and Hon. Sec. of the St. Moritz

Toboggan Club (the Cresta Run).

It has also been said that he commanded his Brigade with great zeal and efficiency! But this was not all.

11

'Vive Les Jeux Olympiques'

'Play the game for the game's sake', 'Play for the side and not for yourself', and 'Do not play to win at all costs' were the tenets of R.J.K., to which might be added '*Mens sana in corpore sano.*'

The Olympic Games had been resurrected by the French Baron Pierre de Coubertin at the end of the last century. When commanding the Base Camp at Antwerp in 1919, my uncle had met the officials who were preparing for the VIIth Olympiad to be held there in the following year. This was just up his street, and he accepted the invitation to be Commandant of the British Team. After it was all over he was elected to the Council of the British Olympic Association (BOA). This body had made Herculean efforts, in spite of public apathy, poor funds and an inferior organization, to send out a team which had, in the event, made a fine impression. A Belgian official had written: 'England has given the world an example of excellent sportsmanship. She must always come to the Games, for without her they would not be Olympic Games.'

My uncle had gone back to Antwerp in 1920 – he was commanding his Territorial Brigade in London by this time – with an open mind. As an amateur of the purest sort, he had wondered whether these gatherings were an aid or a hindrance to international friendship. He returned home, however, with a firm faith in the Olympic Movement and in the missionary work Great Britain had done in showing the world the meaning of true sportsmanship. Some most disgraceful scenes had taken place, chiefly owing to the excitable nature of some Latin nations – they were to occur again in 1924 – but these, he thought, and always thought, were pinpricks in a thoroughly enjoyable meeting. He did blame the world press, though, for purposely fostering the desire to win at all costs by aggravating isolated affairs into international incidents.

By 1921 he had been made Hon. Sec. of the BOA and a member of the International Olympic Committee, which body met in a different country each year and was responsible for the organization of the Games, which were held every four years. In 1922, the year in which he left the Army, he realized that, in spite of public apathy and often downright opposition, it was essential for Great Britain to support her old ally, France, at the 1924 Games in Paris. He therefore called a meeting at the Army and Navy Club, Pall Mall, which was attended by representatives of influential opinion – politicians, sporting pundits and other enthusiasts. It was unanimously agreed that we should send a representative team to Paris, but that it could only be representative if there was a strong British Olympic Association which could ensure proper organization and the procurement of necessary funds.

The BOA was therefore re-organized on a firm basis, with the Duke of Sutherland as President, Earl Cadogan as Chairman of the Council and R.J.K. as Hon. Sec., the last-named to work from new offices at 166 Piccadilly, W1. My uncle always had 'Friends at Court', Private Secretaries or Comptrollers of the Household – people he had doubtless known in his army days – to interest the Royal Family in his ventures. Thus he was able to obtain the Patronage of King George V as well as three of his sons as Vice-Patrons. The social framework of England had not changed much over the years; the Englishman was still reputed to 'love a Lord', although, to a lesser extent than in 1914, and the aristocracy still represented land, power and wealth. To assist the new President a number of Vice-Presidents were enlisted, which included five Marquises, nine Earls, five Viscounts, six Barons, four Baronets, and five Knights, to say nothing of Privy Councillors, MPs and a smattering of Generals and Air Marshals. In addition, Lord Cadogan, Chairman of the Council, now had 56 people, mostly representatives of the various sporting Associations, to advise him.

Here indeed was a formidable collection of 'the Good, the

Great – and the Wealthy' to see that our team for Paris in 1924 was the best available to uphold the standards of the country, which had, indeed, invented many of the sports now available to the world. The only thing now lacking was the money to provide for the expenses of our competitors in what was meant to be a purely amateur contest. In 1923, therefore, Lord Cadogan and my uncle toured Great Britain to appeal for the necessary funds.

No longer having to command a Territorial Brigade or supervise the building of the new Army playing grounds, R.J.K., ensconced in his new office at 166 Piccadilly, was once again in his element. In April 1923 the International Committee met in Rome, the opening ceremony being presided over by the King of Italy and Signor Mussolini. The Italians had made a poor showing at Antwerp, with a handful of badly-equipped and trained young men. On coming to power, however, Mussolini had determined that the Italians must be physically fit for the tasks required of them, and had made the nation sport-conscious. Previous to this, games had been looked on by all classes as something vulgar and brutal, which had made the English mad! The change after three years had been so remarkable that by 1924 Italy was to enter 200 athletes and an even greater number in 1928. But she found it difficult to overcome her innate excitability.

When the Committee met in Rome, two Italians were waiting to be tried for killing the referee of a local football match. R.J.K. wrote:

Included in our programme was a Command to attend a State Ball at the Quirinal. Soon after the dancing had started I was standing with Count Henri de Baillet Latour, President of the IOC, when Mussolini came slowly along and, recognizing the Count, asked how our Congress was getting on. 'And tell me, please,' he asked, 'how do you think we are getting on in sport? Are we making progress?' 'Great progress indeed,' said Count Henri. Then turning to me, Mussolini said, 'We shall never make the same progress as you English.' 'On the contrary, Sir, you have made even greater progress, for I understand you have recently killed a referee! Although we often throw stones at them, we have never killed one yet!' Turning to the Count, he said, 'I do not quite understand,' whereupon the Count, in much better French than mine, repeated

75

what I had said. Fortunately, Mussolini lacked a sense of humour and quite missed the point of the story. Wishing us both good night, he solemnly passed along without a word. Thus ended my only attempt to make the Duce laugh, and now, nearly 20 years later, as Italy surrenders her last Abyssinian fortress, which means the death knell of her African Empire, I doubt whether there is anyone in the world who could make him laugh. In any case, who the devil wants to?

This was in 1943. Two years later, in April 1945, Mussolini and 12 Fascist Party members were executed by their countrymen and dumped in a pile at a petrol station in Milan. They were later strung up head downwards, like carcasses in a butcher's shop. Whatever his faults, Benito had certainly invigorated the Italian people in many respects during the earlier days of his régime – but did this easy-going Latin race want to be invigorated?

45 Countries took part in the VIIIth Olympiad in Paris in 1924. Our much strengthened British Olympic Association had resulted in the raising and training of 10 officials, 300 competitors and 50 trainers. Once again R.J.K. went out as Team Commandant, assisted by the Marquis of Clydesdale, Lieut.-Colonel J. Betts and Lieut. (later Field Marshal Sir) Gerald Templer, who were responsible *inter alia* for accommodation in five hotels and for everything which made for the comfort of all concerned. In addition to all this, my uncle was Hon. Sec. of the BOA, a member of the five-strong Executive Committee of the International Committee and a a member of the five-strong Jury of Honour, the last-named being the adjudicators of any untoward incidents with an international complexion. He might almost have said, '*Les Jeux Olympiques – c'est moi!*' As was said of him in his obituary in *The Times* in 1956, 'His advice was much sought after by representatives of other nations which was always willingly given, usually followed and nearly always proved to be right.'

In Paris the Prince of Wales laid a wreath on the tomb of the French Unknown Soldier, competitors paraded round the arena and the Games opened in classic style. Olympic villages had not yet been introduced, nevertheless the amount of entertaining which took place ensured the success of the Games for future years. A good time was had by all – or nearly all – which was the object of the exercise.

The final results were very creditable, especially in the track events – which always held the limelight. Our runners, after a meticulous training, exceeded all hopes. H.W. Abrahams won the 100 metres after equalling the Olympic Record of 10.6 secs three times in 26 hours. E.H. Liddell was third in the 200 metres and won the 400 metres in 47.4 secs, gaining the World Amateur Record. D.G.A. Lowe won the 800 metres, and H.B. Stallard was third in the 1,500 metres. The heroics and the romanticizing shown in the film about the Paris Olympiad, *Chariots of Fire*, must largely be discounted. There is no evidence that Liddell refused to run on a Sunday on religious grounds, and my uncle appeared under a false name, the only recognizable bit of him being the inevitable cigar stuck in his mouth!

The Olympiad had been marred, nevertheless, by two scandalous incidents in the boxing and fencing finals – relatively insignificant, yet enough to give the Press the excuse to indulge in sensational headlines and to cast further doubt in some minds as to the wisdom of holding the Games at all. My uncle witnessed them both, having to take action as well, being a member of the five-man Jury of Honour to which all serious complaints were brought. Having well-drilled the British team with the rule that 'never was the decision of a referee or judge to be questioned', he could sit back with the fairly safe assurance that he would never have to try his own countrymen. He described the incidents as follows:

In the semi-finals of the Light Weight Boxing, the referee, T.J. Walker – president of our Amateur Boxing Association – had given a fight, quite rightly so, too, in favour of a Belgian against an Italian who had then tried to lay hands on Walker, this performance being backed up by his compatriots, women included, in the audience, who pelted Walker with all they could lay their hands on. T.J. Walker walked out of the Olympic Games, never to return.

In the semi-finals of the Middle Weight an Italian referee then proceeded to give a fight to a Frenchman, du Vallon, against Sgt. Mallin of Great Britain – both amateur champions – despite the fact that du Vallon had bitten Mallin in the left breast, producing a cut which was plain for all to see. On the day following the Americans and the Swedes refused to enter the ring for their finals unless the French Committee agreed to withdraw du Vallon, which it agreed to. When three or four thousand Frenchmen found that it was Sgt. Mallin who entered the ring that night – an announcement should, of course, have been made – pandemonium broke loose and they went completely mad, as only a French crowd can do. Missiles were hurled once again, the crowd started to attack the summoned gendarmes, and when Mallin had won his fight and the Union Jack was raised the spectators went even madder, spitting at the flag and calling out, '*Voleur, voleur*'. Thus ended the Boxing Championships of 1924, amid scenes which have probably never been witnessed before in a boxing ring.

The second incident concerned the fencing, in which eight competitors had got into the final Pool; the one who gained the largest number of fights being the winner. In this final Pool were three Italians including the greatest swordsman of all time in the modern world, Pulitti. And when the Hungarian referee, Kovacs, and his judges noticed that neither of the two Italians had offered the slightest resistance to Pulitti, they disqualified all three for 'squaring' their fights. Pulitti and his two colleagues then tried to assault Kovacs, cheered by their friends in the audience. The next day I was called to the Jury of Honour where I learned that Kovacs, whilst having a drink at the Folies Bergère, had been slapped twice on the face by Pulitti, who had sprung from nowhere and disappeared into the crowd as quickly.

We expelled Pulitti from the Games for ever but this was not the end. On arrival at Turin on their way home, Pulitti had once again performed his Folies Bergère act on the platform, whereupon Kovacs had challenged him to a duel. The two met later in a small village in Hungary where Pulitti wounded his opponent in the arm. Honour being satisfied the two men then embraced each other – and the referee – and the incident was closed, both parting the best of friends. *Vive les Jeux Olympiques! Vive le Sport. Vive tout le monde!*

An aftermath to the Games is provided by one of R.J.K.'s memoirs concerning a luncheon with Count Clary; a 75-year-old bearded aristocrat who was President of the French Olympic Association, which body had been responsible for the organization of the Paris Games. He was also a member of the International Committee.

78

The memoir was called, 'And one of the very best for me!' It went as follows:

I was preparing to leave Paris for England at the end of the Olympiad when Count Clary rang me at my hotel: 'I have some very important news for you. Can you have lunch with me here tomorrow. Just you and I. *Sans façon*! (pot luck). If you can, come at one o'clock "*a l'heure militaire*" (at one sharp)'. So I presented myself at his comfortable flat in the Avenue des Malesherbes for '*un déjeuner sans façons*'.

'So glad you could come. Over lunch we can talk about the little matter which I mentioned to you yesterday.' And taking me into the dining room, he gave me one of the best lunches I had ever had. There was little of the '*sans façon*' about it, and with a bottle of the best claret, a Napoleon brandy and a large cigar, I was feeling on top of my form when my host began:

'It has to do with the decorations which the French Government proposes to give to those members of the British Olympic Association who have helped us so much to make the Games the great success they have been. I propose to recommend that Lord Cadogan and Lord Campden be made Officers and Evan Hunter and Harry Barclay Chevaliers of the French Legion of Honour. And that you, who are an "Officier" already, should be made a Commandeur. Will that be satisfactory to you and your colleagues?'

'I am sure', I said, 'we shall be most honoured.' And filling my glass with another cognac, he continued, 'And on your part I am asking if you would do the same for us!'

Knowing what a difficult thing it was to get our Government to give decorations for sport to even our own people, but not wishing to appear discourteous to the old Count, I said, 'Certainly, I will talk with our Chairman, Lord Cadogan.' 'Thank you,' replied the Count. 'What de Polignac thought you might do would be to give him a very good one, a good one to Frantz Reichel, one not so good to Albert Glandez – and one of the very best to myself!'

'I will certainly do my best for you all,' was my parting shot.

'A thousand thanks – and a thousand thanks for all the help you have given us,' replied the Count; and as I was getting into my taxi he added finally, 'Do not forget the decorations for us – and one of the very best for myself.'

Wonderful people the French, I thought, as the taxi drove me back to my hotel.

* * * * *

There is no evidence that Count Clary or the Marquis de Polignac ever graced the ranks of some British Order of Chivalry or that the Lords Cadogan or Campden ever reinforced the French Legion of Honour. But how cosy, how patrician it all was, so comfortably arranged over a brandy and cigar! Clary and R.J.K. would be turning in their graves today if they realized how the Games have changed in recent years; how commercial they have become in the grip of advertizers and big business; how some nations have gauged their standing in the world by the success of their athletes; how there has been a desire to win at all costs, with the use of drugs if necessary. No longer are they gatherings of amateur sportsmen in friendly rivalry.

With other schemes afoot, my uncle resigned as Hon. Sec., BOA, after the Games in 1924. He attended the 1928 Games in Amsterdam, but only as a member of the International Committee, a body from which he resigned after the Los Angeles Games in 1932, which he did not attend. Berlin in 1936 – a propaganda setting for Adolf Hitler and the Nazis – would have been quite beyond him.

12

'A Proper Toff'

With the Paris Olympiad behind him, this ubiquitous man turned his attention to founding what was his own particular baby, the National Playing Fields Association. Having provided playing grounds for the military, he was now determined to do likewise for the nation. The Association was inaugurated at the Albert Hall, London, in 1925.

By 1925 my uncle, with his cigar and carnation, with his flair for organization and showmanship, with his particular characteristics and personality – not, to be sure, admired by everyone – had become quite a figure in the sporting world. Knowing, moreover, from his service days the private secretaries of the Royal Family, he was able to get their masters to patronize his undertakings, which drew in, as though to a magnet, the wealthy and the powerful.

Moreover, he was gifted with the ability to talk, and be on easy terms with, all sections of society. His restless mind, in addition, was continually churning out new ideas: articles for the Press, advice to Field Marshals or politicians, campaigns for this and that; some of which was his own business, much of which was not. Since he was a boy he was afraid of the dark, to the extent that he always kept the light on at night. This was perhaps one of the causes of his copious writing. Chambermaids had long given up the idea of tidying his bedroom, so littered was it with piles of correspondence or sheets of quarto paper which were the result of a night's work. As he grew into old age, his script had developed into a series of wavy squiggles which only close relatives and the unfortunate woman who did his typing could decipher.

In the early days of the Second World War he spent an evening at the Dorchester Hotel during the nightly blitz with the well-known *Daily Mail* reporter, G. Ward Price, and Major General J.F.C. Fuller, military critic and an old friend of his. After a long session of reminiscences Ward Price suggested that he should put his anecdotes on paper for possible publication. In the course of time over a hundred 'memories' were committed to paper, but that was as far as they got – his impulsive mind was always distracted by new ideas. They have lain in my roof since his death in 1956. The following may reveal not only his own character but life as it was led in the twenties of this century.

'A Proper Toff!'

A friend of mine, whom I had first met in Antwerp during the 1920 Olympiad, asked me to present the prizes at the Burnham (Bucks) Athletic Sports Club on August Bank Holiday. The village green on my arrival was thronged with four or five hundred spectators lining the track, with a band playing in the middle. There was an interval for tea, and so I decided to walk round the ground to look at the villagers enjoying themselves.

I noticed a little group of boys who, in fact, turned out to be all Cockneys, and I heard one of them say, 'Gor blimey, 'Arry, there's a toff! Wonder what 'e wears on Sunday!' I was wearing an ordinary summer suiting at the time and I had a carnation in my button hole. Perhaps I did look a bit of a swell! However, turning round immediately, I said, 'The suit I've got on! It's the only one I have, and I sleep in it too, spats and all.'

To which 'Arry replied: 'Wevver yer sleeps in it, guvner, or wevver ye don't, all I can say is that yer a proper toff! Ain't he, mates?'

As I continued my walk I thought to myself: 'There's no one in the world like a Cockney for humour!'

'Harry Curr of Notting Hill'

In the early twenties I had been to Germany and had been impressed by the craze for sport and the way the natives, once so corpulent and stodgy, were able to shed their clothes for outdoor activities. I did not exactly condone the nudity that was practised, but on my return to England I gave a broadcast on the subject from 2 LO – then at Savoy Hill – and also took up the cudgels on behalf of one Harry Curr of Notting Hill. This unfortunate youth had been fined by a magistrate for sun-bathing on the Lido in Kensington Gardens in a pair of football shorts, i.e. exposing his body without the apparent intent to bathe. Instead of branding the boy as something unclean, the magistrate should have fined him but made it quite clear that he considered the law to be ridiculous. That, at any rate, was what I myself thought to be the right course. I suggested the formation of an anti-Mrs Grundy League which would help to sweep away the restrictions and pruderies of a past age. (Mrs Grundy was a mythical figure at that time who, embodying propriety and prudery, stalked around with her umbrella, denouncing the abominations of the devil.)

'Zeal at Deal'
In the summer of 1924 the *Evening Standard* offered £500 for the first person to swim from France to England, and shortly afterwards this handsome prize was won by an Italian, Orlando. The presentation was made at a luncheon at the Savoy Hotel, at which I was an honoured guest. After it was all over I was introduced to Orlando by his manager, Bariati, and I asked the latter, whose English was not too good, what sort of reception Orlando had had on the shore at Deal where he had landed quite naked, his costume having become torn and detached on the way over.

'Ah, *Generale*,' said Bariati, 'ze crowd was formidable and varee enthusiastico, but poor Orlando 'ee receive varee big shock because one of your poleeceman com up with 'ees pencil and leetle book, and 'e say, "You geeve me your name and ware you leeve because you expose all zee person to zee crowd, and zat ees against zee law of England." And ven eet ees all ovair I take 'eem to zee hotel, and aftair good sleep 'ees friends geeve 'eem a partee, and in telling zee storee of 'ow 'ee kom to your Deal, Orlando, 'ee take zee top of zee little fingair of 'ees right 'and with zee thumb and forefinger of zee left, and showing 'eet to 'ees friends 'ee say, "But it was so stupeed and so unnecessarie of zee policeman to make all zee fuss because, aftair nearly 20 hours in zee varee cold watair, eet was only as beeg as zat."

'The All-Blacks Luncheon'
In January 1925 I organized, at short notice and at the instigation of the *Evening Standard*, a farewell luncheon at the Piccadilly Hotel, W1, given by the sportsmen of the Motherland to the All-

Blacks rugger team from New Zealand, which had won all its 30 matches.

It should be said that during the match against England one of the All-Blacks had been sent off the field by the referee, and that many people considered he had been very hardly dealt with. Consequently I had the greatest difficulty in persuading him to attend the lunch, which could not have been held without his presence. The Prince of Wales was coming, and I had written to Lord Lonsdale asking him to take the chair, an invitation he accepted with pleasure. A letter had also gone, *inter alia,* to Lord Desborough, asking him to be a host – and he had replied, 'Delighted to come and take the chair.' So a coin had to be tossed, which came down in favour of Desborough. Lord Lonsdale was written to, and he sent a cheque for £10 with a promise of more if requested.

And so there assembled in the lounge of the hotel the greatest gathering of British sportsmen – over 300 of them – ever seen in London, every single sport being represented by past or present champions. The lunch went off perfectly, and everyone was in fine fettle when the Prince of Wales rose to propose the toast to the All-Blacks. 'Fellow sportsmen,' he began, 'I'm sorry to tell you I've had a rotten lunch – but only because I knew I had to make a speech at the end of it!' The Piccadilly chef, who had come up to hear the speeches and who had entirely missed the point, fell down in a dead faint and had to be carried out!

The next incident, which was very far from humorous, occurred when Lord Lonsdale was proposing the toast of the chairman, Lord Desborough. 'I feel, first of all,' he began, 'that I must say a word on the subject no one has mentioned: the sending off the field of one of the All-Blacks.' And, without realizing that he had never made a bigger *faux pas* – for the lunch was being given to bury the incident – he went on to explain how we must always 'play the game'. However, there it was. Next day he wrote, 'I don't think I've ever seen anything like the luncheon yesterday. It was wonderful. I think I was right to say a word about playing the game. Nobody else had! I enclose another tenner. I'm sure you'll want it!'

'What a Peach' [or Dilly-dallying with a Contessa]
In September 1924 I was staying in Menaggio in Italy on the shores of Lake Como. How lovely Menaggio and all those other villages are, such as Bellagio, Cadenabbia, Locarno, Tremezzo,

Bellinzona, Pallanza and Poriezza. I was having a game of golf one day with an old friend of mine, Douglas Fairbanks [senior], and looking at the lakes and the mountains all around us, he said, 'You know, I've been to all the most beautiful places in the world but I've never seen anything as beautiful as this.' And he meant it.

Those were the days when the Italians were beginning to become keen on golf, and amongst them was a lovely young Italian girl with blonde hair, the Contessa Antonietta Rivolta, who, that year, had been runner-up in the Italian Women's Championship. She was very much in demand, so having been introduced to her, we had several games together – and I spent many days at her lovely villa, sunbathing or skimming over the lake in a speedboat.

I wanted, when playing golf with her, to express my admiration of her skill in the Italian language. It occurred to me to say to her after she had played a fine stroke. 'A peach of a shot, Antonietta! A real peach,' as we might have said in England. So one evening, in my hotel, I looked up my English-Italian conversation book and found '*Che pesca!* What a peach!' Next day we drove off from the first tee and she subsequently played a beautiful mashie shot, so I called out:

'*Che pesca,* Antonietta! *Che pesca.*' She took no notice. At the next hole, after another fine shot, I repeated: '*Che pesca,* Antonietta! *Che pesca.*' Again she took no notice. At the third hole she started off with a fine drive, so I said, once again: '*Che pesca,* Antonietta! *Che pesca.*'

'Why you keep saying to me "*Che pesca*?" What does it mean?'

'Because in England,' I said, 'a peach is the most beautiful, the most expensive, the most rare and the most delicious fruit we have. So when I say "What a peach!", we mean a very fine shot!'

'But,' she replied, 'here in Italy peaches are as common as potatoes, so you might just as well say to me "*Che patata,* Antonietta! *Che patata."* And I do not like you to tell me that my strokes are potatoes!'

'Will you please forgive me, Antonietta, I'm terribly sorry. '

'You are forgiven – but do not do it again, please.'

That was my first and last attempt to pay a compliment in Italian to my lovely Antonietta.

'A Couple of Generals' [or Down to Earth]
Some years ago, in the 1920s, I happened to be staying at the Links Hotel, Thurlestone, in South Devon. The village then consisted of

a single street of picturesque cottages, but the Hotel, of modern construction, lay outside the village. It could be reached by a winding track across the sand dunes and was perched all by itself on the cliff edge overlooking the sea.

One evening I had been to Kingsbridge, about five miles away at the head of the Salcombe Estuary, and was returning to Thurlestone by bus. Apart from the conductor, the only other occupant was a stout middle-aged woman of the working classes, poor but respectable. She had with her a bag and a large parcel. On reaching Thurlestone the conductor helped her and her baggage out of the bus, saying, 'This is as far as we go, mum. Take the road to your left, and at the bottom, by the Golf Club, you'll find the track. Follow that and you'll come to the Links Hotel. It's about a quarter of a mile's walk.' Whereupon he said 'Good night' and disappeared into the pub.

It was a very wild night, very dark and raining hard. The woman looked extremely miserable so I said to her, 'I'm going to the Links Hotel, so I can show you the way, if you like.'

'Thank you very much, sir. It's very kind of you.' So taking up her bag, leaving her with the parcel, off we went to find the track across the sand dunes. Curious to know what was taking her to the Links Hotel at that time of night, I asked her.

'Oh!' she said, 'I'm a general, sir, a cook general. I've been engaged by the Hotel, and I start work tomorrow, sir.'

'What a coincidence,' I said.

'Why is that, sir?' she asked.

'Because I am a General too. So here we are, a couple of Generals. Take my arm, you'll find it easier.'

So a pair of perfectly good Generals went arm in arm across the sand dunes until we arrived safely at the Hotel. This we entered through the front door into the lounge, where the guests were waiting for dinner, still arm in arm with our bundles by our sides, looking very wet and bedraggled. The manager came out of his office and was very surprised to see us standing like that in the lounge.

'A couple of perfectly good Generals,' I said. 'All present and correct. After an arduous and very trying night march across the sand dunes, we should like a drink on the house.' So I marched my brother General to the bar where the manager, who had been expecting his 'General' since midday, was only too pleased to signal her safe arrival by standing us a couple of doubles!

86

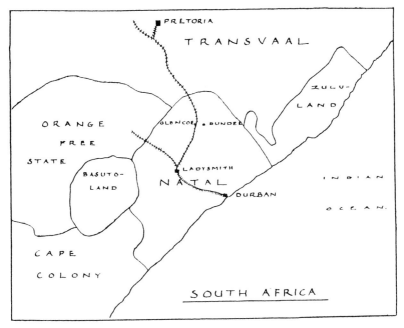

R.J.K. as a Captain and ADC to Major General H.M. Lawson, GOC 2nd Division, Aldershot, c. 1910

R.J.K. when commanding the 76th Infantry brigade, 1916

R.J.K. standing between their Majesties King George V and Queen Mary at an Army Cup Final in Aldershot

'What they've got.'

'What we're out to get for them.'

From the programme of the Inaugural Meeting of the National Playing Fields
Association at the Royal Albert Hall, London, on 8 July 1925

In later years

Field Marshal Sir Gerald Templer, CIGS and Colonel, the Royal Irish Fusiliers, unveiling a memorial to R.J.K. in the Aldershot Stadium in 1957

* * * * *

My uncle was entirely at home with Kings and Princes – but did not lack the common touch!

13

Playing Grounds For All

The year 1925 saw the birth of what my uncle liked to call his child: The National Playing Fields Association. On his own initiative as a young Captain in 1908, he had brought into being the scheme for providing the military garrisons in the UK with an abundance of playing fields where hardly any had existed before; a scheme which he was to supervise personally up to 1914 and again in the post-war years, in addition to his normal duties. It was while going round the country during the latter period that he realized that young people in the cities and large towns were as badly off for recreational facilities as the soldier had been prior to 1908. It was calculated that our Public Schools had, on average, one acre of playing grounds for every 30 boys, whereas many boroughs in the country as a whole had less than one acre for 25,000 inhabitants. This, thought R.J.K., was disastrous for the future health of the nation. He also found that 63% of those offering themselves as army recruits were rejected on medical grounds, over and above the 10% who never reached the doctors, having been immediately rejected by the recruiting sergeants beforehand.

During the preceding century towns and cities had multiplied in size beyond all previous conceptions. In the absence of planning authorities, no thought had been given to sports grounds, so that suburban estates and industrial areas had spread unchecked. Worst of all were the rows of industrial workers' dwellings, back to back with a narrow street in between. It was on these streets that the young people had to play their games of cricket or football. As they got older they could be seen hanging round street corners with a fag dangling from their lips – or going off to watch the local team play in the stadium. Watching professionals play was definitely not my uncle's idea of spending a Saturday afternoon; our youths should be developing their bodies by participating themselves. This conception generally fell on deaf ears, but my uncle's conviction that young people did indeed want to take part was driven home by a scene he had witnessed at Newcastle.

He had been invited by John McKenna, President of the Football League, to watch Newcastle United playing Aston Villa on their home ground, but he did not stay long and went off to see the Newcastle Town Moor, where other matches were being played. And on the fringe of the Moor was a game being played by small boys who were using their coats as goalposts. He noted that the boy playing outside-left only had a boot on his left foot. 'Where's your other boot?' he asked. 'Bert's got that. It's like this, y'see; we've only gotta pair of foota boots 'tween us. 'E 'as right boot as outside-right: I 'as 'tuther as outside left.' That, considered R.J.K., was absolute proof that the younger generations wanted to play games and not just watch League matches in their spare time.

At the end of his time at Malvern College he had taken a football team to Canning Town, E17, to play against a team of boys from the Dockland Settlements, Malvern's Mission in the East End of London. Afterwards he saw the conditions under which the boys existed. 'Fortunately,' he wrote, 'I saw the picture for myself and I have never forgotten it to this day or allowed it out of my mind.' Now, about 30 years later, he saw his chance to do something about a state of affairs which had not improved with time. His aim was to try to provide open spaces on a basis of five acres per 1000 inhabitants; rather optimistic it might be thought, since it was far too late in most areas. So to bring an Association into being he had to resign his commission in the Army. By 1922 he was a Brigadier General at the age of 46, and he might have gone much further up the ladder – or he might not have done, considering his propensity for rubbing his superiors up the wrong way!

The founding of a National Association was a praiseworthy idea but where did one start? There was no Army Council or ASCB on this occasion; no General or kindly Colonel to say, 'put down tha musket, lad, and dig!' He had to find his own 'top brass' to sponsor the organization, interest the various sporting and phi-lanthropic bodies, weld together the few existing entities, such as the London and the Manchester Playing Fields Societies – who did not much want to be welded – and, last but by no means least, raise some cash.

He found his 'top brass' in St. James's Palace. The Movement was started, R.J.K. claimed, on 6 October, 1921.

'I was driving back to the Palace with the Duke of York and his equerry, Basil Brooke, after watching a football match on the Spurs Ground between that team and the Corinthians in aid of the Dockland Settlements and Malvernian Mission in Canning Town, in which I was interested. I told the Duke of my scheme to form a National Association to deal with the lack of playing facilities in the country generally. Seeming most interested, he told me to for-ward my ideas in writing. Some weeks later I was summoned to the Palace, as the Prince of Wales and the Duke wanted to see me – Prince Henry, I rather think, was there too. The Duke thought the Prince ought to take the scheme up and be President, but the latter said he had not got the time and that 'Bertie would make a much better job of it.' From that moment the Duke of York agreed to sponsor and become President of the National Association when formed.

With the pressing needs of the 1924 Olympiad and the completion of the Garrison schemes still be considered – and he was still com-manding a Territorial Brigade until 1922 – the idea passed into the back of my uncle's mind until, in 1923, the White City Stadium came on to the market. With a view to provide an open space for the children of West London he talked it over with certain people, and the Prince of Wales agreed to attend the first rally there, pro-vided it was powerfully sponsored – but the idea never took shape.

The Paris Olympiad successfully over, R.J.K. invited a selec-tion of powerful enthusiasts to a meeting at the Army and Navy Club, W1 – exactly as he had done for the British Olympic Association in 1922 – to consider the founding of a National Playing Fields Association. This was formed in embryo, with the Duke of Sutherland as President; Sir Arthur Crosfield, Bart, Chairman; Sir Thomas Inskip (later Viscount Caldecote), and (later Sir) Noel Curtis Bennett, Hon. Treasurer. The last-named became Chairman in 1940 and combined that office with the Hon. Treasureship until his death in 1950. R.J.K. wrote:

> The plan of campaign was to issue a letter to the Press signed by 32 influential people; this was followed up by taking a party of reporters to Aldershot, where everything was running smoothly, then to London dockland with its crying need for open spaces. The next step was to win the co-operation of the existing Societies; so in April 1925 I addressed, under the chairmanship of the Earl of Meath, the Metropolitan Public Gardens Association, the London Playing Fields Society and the Commons and Footpath Preservation Society. They were not at all keen to be absorbed into a parent organization, but so great had been the response to our larger appeal that they had no option but to come in.

The National Playing Fields Association was officially inaugurated at the Royal Albert Hall on 8 July 1925, in the presence of the Duke and Duchess of York and the Prime Minister, Mr Ramsay MacDonald. The Duke had accepted the invitation to become President, a post he held until his accession to the throne as King George VI, when he became Patron, passing the Presidency to Earl Mountbatten and then to Philip, Duke of Edinburgh. To a fully packed Hall the Band of the Coldstream Guards played suitable airs, there were speeches by 17 eminent politicians and sportsmen and a resolution was passed that 'This Meeting pledges to support the efforts of the NPFA to provide and encourage the provision of adequate facilities for open-air recreation in and around every city, town and village in the country.'

This was my uncle's great day; the fulfilment of his wish: the NPFA had come to life. At long last, he hoped, our young people would no longer have to play their games in the gutters of our industrial slums.

The general idea was that each County should form its own Association, for it was felt that, being a voluntary movement, people would rather give money and gifts of land to their own neighbourhood rather than to a central body. My uncle, therefore, had the task of visiting the Lords Lieutenant to encourage the formation of such Associations, as well as to solicit gifts of money for the movement in general. Great assistance was given by King George V, who took the unprecedented step of writing to each Lord Lieutenant beforehand. R.J.K. was greatly encouraged by being able to collect in Scotland from the Carnegie Trust a cheque for the, then considerable, sum of £250,000.

By July 1927 the NPFA had an Executive Committee of 50 advised by a Council of representatives from 150 organizations in the Country, sporting, municipal, county and philanthropic. The Prince of Wales had broadcast an appeal which had brought in £330,000 as well as gifts of land. And then the whole thing went wrong – or at least it did for R.J.K. personally. He resigned as Honorary Organizing Secretary. He had never been afraid to criticize his superiors if he considered they were in the wrong, he had always had a dislike of Councils or Committees; he liked things to go his way or not at all. On this occasion there was friction between himself and some members of the Executive Committee who wished to bring him to heel. Very conveniently, the Association was to be incorporated as a Company, not working for profit, under Royal Charter and, furthermore, a new Constitution was to be written. So it was decided to make my uncle a Paid, instead of Honorary, Organizing Secretary. But he felt that he could not become the paid servant of an Association which would never have seen the light of day if it had not been for him. So, much as he would have liked the money, he resigned. 'Congratulations on doing the big thing,' wired C. Wreford Brown, an old friend of his and a member of the Committee.

To save everyone's face, he was voted an honorarium of £750 and made a Life Member of the Association, an honour which had only been bestowed as yet on a very few eminent people. Thus he severed his connection with the official running of the NPFA. Used as he was, in his impetuous way, to jumping from one thing to another, this was a particular blow from which he never really recovered. He had overplayed his hand at long last. A Press release was distributed, announcing his resignation on account of his heavy involvement with the Olympic Games and other activities.

Thus he disappeared from this particular scene until 1948, a period of 21 years, by which time all those whom he termed his enemies were dead. Embittered that the credit for the founding of the NPFA had been claimed by others, he communicated with the Chairman, Sir Noel Curtis Bennett. As a result, Sir Noel invited him to the Silver Jubilee Dinner at the Mansion House, where he was seated at the top table and specially welcomed as the 'Founder of the Association'. In 1950 he attended the Annual General Meeting at Caxton Hall, Westminster. Accorded a place on the platform, Sir Noel specially referred to him as 'the man who had conceived the idea of the Association'. At long last he had been recognized as such, an honour claimed by others during the wilderness years. Honour was at last satisfied, but it was all too late.

The President, Philip, Duke of Edinburgh, was represented at his memorial service in 1956.

14

The IXth Olympiad

Regretfully freed from any responsibility for the National Playing Fields, R.J.K. turned this thoughts towards the IXth Olympiad, to be held in Amsterdam in 1928. This he attended, not as Team Commandant this time, but as Vice-Chairman of the British Olympic Association and a member of the International Committee. Nothing has survived in his memoirs of this Meeting, except a rather bizarre story which might well be called:

Foul Play Below Decks
The incidents I am about to tell occurred in the final of the Water Polo Championships which took place in Amsterdam in August 1928, in the presence of the Prince Consort, husband of Queen Wilhelmina. Also present were myself and my colleagues on the International Committee, Lords Rochdale and Aberdare.

The finalists were the Dutch team and the German team. The match in question turned out, as indeed everybody knew it would, to be an extremely rough game – battle would be a better name for it – between the two teams of very powerful men, equally matched in weight and strength, and, judging from what went on from start to finish, without either team showing the slightest regard for the rules!

Consequently the match just developed into a dogfight, there never being a moment when both sides had their full complement of players in the water, so frequently did the Referee have to order first one man and then another out of the 'pool' for glaring breaches of the rules.

For those who do not know the game of Water Polo, it may not be out of place if I say that, provided the players observe the rules and 'play the game', it is a very fine game both for players and spectators alike; a statement, which, I suppose, applies to almost all games.

Whereas in the majority of games the breaking of the rules and the players not 'playing the game' lead to no dire results, the same cannot be said of Water Polo, where players can do each other very serious injury; the unfortunate part about it being that the worst of the foul and dirty play goes on under the water and is, therefore, unseen by the Referee.

This, I regret to say, is exactly what happened in this particular match, the players on both sides – the Dutch being neither better nor worse than the Germans, and vice versa – committing the most unmentionable fouls on each other under the water. Those of us, who were present at the match and saw what went on, and were subsequently present at the meeting of the International Olympic Committee at Lausanne in 1930, when, as the sequel to this story tells, Lord Rochdale proposed that Water Polo should be taken out of the programme, were all agreed that he was fully justified in making the comments he did.

However, the game, or rather the 'dogfight', came to an end with the Germans victorious. As they left the water, the whole assembly to the number of about 5,000 jeered and whistled until they had disappeared into their dressing room. I am quite sure everybody felt relieved when this fresh exhibition of the 'friendly spirit', which International Sport is supposed to engender between nations, came to an end!

* * * * *

The Sequel

In June 1930 the International Committee met in Lausanne, under the Presidency of Count Henri de Baillet Latour; also present were Lords Rochdale and Aberdare, myself and about 30 members of the Committee.

The International Olympic Committee, which, before the present War met in a different Capital in Europe, Asia or Africa every year to transact its business, was meeting this year in its 'home town' Lausanne. I call it its 'home town', because it was in Lausanne that the Frenchman, Baron Pierre de Coubertin, first conceived the idea of bringing to life again the Ancient Olympic Games. To commemorate the occasion the Municipality of Lausanne had presented to the President, to be the Headquarters of the International Olympic Committee for all time, part of a building which belonged to it which went by the name of Mon Repos. It was here that we all assembled on this particular occasion to hold our Annual Congress.

For some time past complaints had been coming in from smaller countries – and from some of the bigger ones too – that, with the constant addition of new events to the Programme, they were finding it increasingly difficult to find the funds to clothe, feed and pay the travelling expenses, to and from wherever the Games were being held, of the number of athletes they had to send, if they wished to be represented in every event – and they all did – in the Programme.

Consequently a letter had been sent to every member of the Committee, drawing his attention to the matter and asking him to come to Lausanne prepared to put forward suggestions for reducing the expenses of the Games, either by cutting out some of the events or by any other means they might suggest.

And so it was that, on the first morning of the Session, our President, rising to his feet, first welcomed us to Lausanne, and then said: 'And now, gentlemen, as you will all see from the "Agenda" you have in front of you, we are going to commence our meeting by discussing this most important question of the reduction of the Programme, and according to our rule I call our German friend and colleague, Herr Lewald, to give us his views.'

Immediately up got Herr Lewald, massive and ponderous in build, standing well over six feet, with close-cropped hair – in fact just a typical Prussian, and this is what he said: 'Mr President, my two colleagues, His Highness Duke Adolphe of Mecklenburgh-Schwerin and Herr Ritter von Anhalt, and I have discussed the matter very earnestly with the different sporting organizations in Germany. We have come to Lausanne definitely agreed that the simplest way to reduce expenses is to eliminate all team games from the Programme, except,' he said, 'Water Polo, for by so doing much expense will be saved, as it is the team games like Football, Hockey, Rowing, Lacrosse, Gymnastics, with their big teams, which cost the countries so much money. I have suggested keeping Water Polo* because it is such a splendid game and, the teams

---

* Germany was the holder of this particular Olympic Championship, and I have no doubt that this was his and his colleagues' reason for wishing to retain Water Polo in the Programme, and not the one he gave out at the meeting.

96

being only five a side, it adds very little to the expense. And, say ing this, Herr Lewald resumed his seat.

Immediately, and without a word of warning and out of his turn, up jumped Lord Rochdale: 'Mr President,' he said, 'I must ask you to excuse me for speaking out of my turn, but our views in England are so diametrically opposed to those just put forward by my friend and colleague, Herr Lewald, that I felt I must intervene at once and state what those views are,' and, before the President could stop him, he went straight on.

'In England we attach the very greatest importance to team games, as opposed to individual games, for they instil into our youth that team spirit which is so essential. I know that I am expressing the views of my fellow-countrymen when I tell you that, sooner than see team games taken out of the Programme, we, in England, would much sooner see the Olympic Games come to an end altogether!!

'I therefore move,' he said, 'that all team games, except Water Polo, be kept in the Programme, and the only reason why I have made an exception in the case of Water Polo is that, because it is such a foul game, after each match there are, I understand, always two or three players on each side who have been so badly mauled that the value of their services to their respective countries, so far as increasing the population is concerned, is absolutely NIL!!!' Having said this, his Lordship resumed his seat.

Immediately there came laughter – much laughter – from the Americans and Scandinavians, all of whom understood and spoke English well, and who saw the humour of Lord Rochdale's words, but not a sound or movement of any kind from the non English-speaking representatives, none of whom had the slightest idea what he had said, or what all the laughter was about!

And it was not until after I had explained the joke to the Marquis de Polignac, who was sitting on my left, and he in turn passed it on to his colleague, Count Clary, who then in turn passed it on to his neighbour, that in the end the whole assembly were enjoying it! – or at any rate, as well as those who have no sense of humour – and that, I am afraid, applied to the majority of my colleagues on the International Olympic Committee – can enjoy a joke.

The motion to eliminate team games from the Programme was defeated, and we found other ways and means of reducing expenses.

* * * * *

That was all he wrote for posterity, but he often told the story of how an opulent looking gentleman with a carnation and smoking a large cigar was buttonholed by the Prince Consort of the Netherlands at a party and touched for a loan of money! The husband of Queen Wilhelmina had no idea that his potential benefactor was just as broke as he was, for R.J.K., for all his opulent appearance, was financially embarrassed. On leaving the Army in 1922 he had commuted half his pension; he had spent the last six years living on the capital sum thus raised, eked out by the remaining annual increment. He had spent all his time, money and enthusiasm on the Olympic Games and the NPFA in an honorary capacity. The advent of the Slump in 1929, which was to last for three years, made matters worse. My uncle had been left a tiny share in the family firm of W. H. Hayden & Co. Ltd. His father had thought, 'Oh, Reggie! He will rise to dizzy heights in the Army.' So he had left the great bulk of the business to his other children. For three years the firm had to pass its dividends, and Reggie was now left in dire straits, supported largely by my father.

In 1932 he accepted a post with the Dorchester and Gordon Hotels under Sir Francis Towle; his monetary affairs now took a decided turn for the better.

15

The Forced Balls of the Hare

During his earlier days R.J.K. had made a great many contacts and friends, which was recognized as a valuable asset by the (newly opened) Dorchester and Gordon Hotels. He was thus deemed to be a fit person to persuade individuals and organizations to hold their private and public celebrations in the hotel group. By 1938 he had, indeed, brought in half a million pounds worth of business – a good deal of money in those days. He now had a suite of rooms at the Dorchester, money to spend, and the run of his teeth in some of the best restaurants and grill rooms in London. At the age of 56 he entered the unreal world of Maharajahs and Hollywood stars, succumbing easily to the round of entertainment and expensive living to be found in the lush hotels in the 1930s. As he wrote later, 'I felt I was losing my grip if I got to bed occasionally before 4.30 a.m.' At an age when life should have been easier, he gave his interior economy a drubbing such as it had not yet experienced.

R.J.K. was both a gourmet and a gourmand, knowing what was what in haute cuisine yet appreciating the humble kipper. He had always done himself proud, yet had been ever mindful of seeing that his soldiers got the best rations which could be obtained for them. When, in 1940, Ward Price of the *Daily Mail* urged him to write some of his experiences for publication, a typescript was duly produced called '100 Incidents in My Life'; but never reaching the typewriter stage was a story which may have been written in bed during the night (he never turned the light off) – an almost indecipherable pencil scrawl with many deletions and alterations.

99

An attempt is made here to reproduce this tale, which has three parts and is all about food in the Gordon Hotels in 1935/36.

'The Bridal Chamber without a Bride'
Part One
Just before Christmas 1935 I was about to have lunch in the Mayfair Hotel, before going off to Ranelagh for a game of golf, when in came an old friend of mine, Sir Park Goff MP, so we arranged to have lunch together. Going straight away in to the Grill Room we were welcomed by Ludr, the head waiter, an Austrian and a real good fellow.

'What have you got today that is ready?' I asked him.

'A lovely roast turkey *à l'Anglaise* and a very delicious jugged hare,' he replied.

We both decided to have the turkey. So off went Ludr, and in a moment up came the carver, wheeling in front of him a trolley on which the turkey rested, and he started to carve two portions.

Park Goff (PG) said, 'Give me plenty of stuffing please, I'm very fond of it.' And then I saw the carver turn to Ludr, who was standing nearby, and say something in an undertone, which seemed to upset him for a moment; then, coming over to our table, he said to PG, 'I'm sorry, sir, but this is Saturday, and the chef never stuffs a turkey on Saturday.'

I should mention here that one of PG's pet aversions was the for-eign element in our English hotels. He was always telling me that, if he had his own way, he wouldn't have a single foreigner, whether he be manager, chef or waiter, in any hotel in the country. His view was that they were nearly all of them potential spies and therefore a positive danger. Furthermore, every one of them kept a perfectly good Englishman out of a job; with which views I found myself in complete agreement. Directly Ludr made the inane and insane excuse about the chef not stuffing turkeys on Saturday, PG, who had a very quick temper and could be in a particularly irascible frame of mind if the occasion demanded, lost his temper com-pletely and said, 'Just like you d—d foreigners. Not one of you ever knows how to cook an English dish. Not one of you can ever tell the truth and, on top of it all, you are all a lot of —— liars.'

Poor Ludr completely collapsed and murmured, 'I'm very sorry, my Lord' – he lost his head and called him Milord when he was only a common Knight – 'If I had known you were coming to lunch I would have seen that the turkey was stuffed.' This made things worse; PG finally blurted out: 'Well, take the d—d turkey away, for I won't eat turkey without stuffing.' So off went the turkey with its tail – if it had one – right between its legs in silence and in great contrast to its arrival a few moments before!

'What may I get you, my Lord?' to which *I* said, 'We'd better have the jugged hare, as it is ready.' So up came the jugged hare with all the pomp and ceremony which had heralded the turkey's arrival.

Ludr was serving a nice helping onto PG's plate when the latter, still very angry about the stuffing, suddenly said: 'Where are the forced meat balls? I can't see any.' This time Ludr was completely knocked out because, as he told me afterwards, he had never heard of such things. I am quite sure he hadn't, and I doubted if the chef or any other foreigner had either.

'I'm sorry, my Lord,' said Ludr, 'but I do not know these forced balls. I will ask the chef.' I was afraid PG was going to have a fit, so purple in the face did he get, so I said: 'Well, PG, it is no use waiting for Ludr to ask the chef, who has probably never heard of such things, so we had better get on with our lunch since we are both in a hurry.' We had just finished when Ludr came through the swing doors bearing a plate on which were four little balls!

'Here, my Lord, I have the hare's forced balls; two for my Lord and two for the General.'

'No, I've finished my lunch, take the d—d things away.'

'No, PG,' I said, 'you must eat them now, as the chef has made them specially for us.'

PG picked one up on his fork and put it into his mouth, spitting it out almost immediately, saying, 'D—d sausage meat. Take them away.' That was the end of Ludr and his forced hare's meat balls, as he was calling them at the end; so bewildered was he after all the trouble he had taken to get 'my Lord' all he wanted.

On the following Monday I thought it right to bring this to the notice of the Managing Director, Sir Francis Towle. So, on arriving at my office in the Metropole Hotel, where the central offices of the Gordon Hotels were situated, I sent a memo, through my secretary, to Sir Francis. Explaining the incident in the Mayfair Hotel two days ago, I finished up with the following:

'I think it important that you should be told of this incident because I have heard complaints from different quarters. My own opinion, for what it is worth, is that roast turkey without stuffing, roast beef without Yorkshire pudding, boiled silverside without dumplings, saddle of mutton without redcurrant jelly, boiled leg of mutton without caper sauce and jugged hare without forced meat balls is exactly the same as a bridegroom in the bridal chamber on his wedding night – but without a bride!'

Half an hour or so later, Sir Francis asked if I would go along to see him for a few minutes. I found the great man being very pompous and extremely angry – not with me but with, what he called, his bloody fool chefs. Whereupon he dictated a letter to all his managers and chefs, explaining that English people expected their turkey to be stuffed and their jugged hare to have forced meat balls, etc. etc. So, thanking me for bringing this to his notice, I duly returned to my office.

So ended the story of the turkey which wasn't stuffed and the jugged hare which was served without forced meat balls. But there were two sequels to this, which I will relate.

Part Two

A few days later – again just before Christmas – I invited Sir Harold Bowden, the bicycle king and chairman of the British Olympic Association, to have lunch with me in the Restaurant at the Dorchester Hotel. I had previously warned Sartori, the Italian head waiter, about this. We had just sat down and were trying to make up our minds what to eat when up came old Cigolini, who had just come from the Palace Hotel in Biarritz to be the hotel manager. After greeting us he said, 'General, we have roast turkey on the menu today.' And, with the suspicion of a smile on his face, he continued, 'We have followed Sir Francis's instructions and stuffed it well, so you will not find much cause for complaint.'

We both decided to have the turkey; so while the waiter went off to get it, I told Sir Harold what had happened when I lunched with Sir Park Goff a few days previously at the Mayfair. I had just finished when up came Sartori, followed by a carver pushing in front of him a brand new roast turkey. So far it had been untouched by the carver's knife and was as intact as the proverbial maiden. Bringing up the rear came Cigolini – the whole as fine a cortège as one could wish to see! Directly I saw it, I noticed that it wasn't like the ordinary turkeys one was accustomed to see with beautiful lines – streamlined, in fact. No! This one was all out of shape. The chef had certainly carried out Sir Francis Towle's orders and stuffed it well; so well indeed that he had stuffed it fore and aft and on both flanks so that it was literally bulging with sage, sausage meat and chestnut. It was almost impossible to see the turkey for stuffing! 'There!' said Cigolini, 'If you are satisfied, I hope you will tell Sir Francis how well the chef has carried out his instructions.'

Then Cigoloni went on, 'Tell me, please, about these "Forced Balls of the Hare". Neither the chef nor anyone in the kitchen nor I nor anyone I have asked about these "Balls of the Forced Hare" has ever heard of them. Tell me, please, how they are made, and I will tell the chef.'

'You haven't quite got the name right,' I said, 'Forced meat balls is the correct name. But I don't expect any Frenchman or Italian knows what they are, yet all English cooks know. So I'll ask my sister, who has a good plain cook, for a recipe.'

Which brings me to the sequel to this.

Part Three

Having obtained a recipe from my sister, I sent it to Cigolini, who passed it on to his head chef with orders that '*bals forcés*', as he now insisted on calling them, should always be served with jugged hare. A few days later I had a small party for lunch at the Dorchester; this time in the Grill Room, which most people preferred for both lunch and dinner, to the Restaurant. There was an exceedingly charming head waiter, an Italian named Mastosi.

I had told him two or three days before that I was giving this party, mentioning that my sister, whom he knew well, would be coming. So, as we were sitting down at the table, Mastosi said, 'We have a great surprise for you and your friends today. We have jugged hare on the menu made specially by the chef.' And, turning to my sister, he added. 'With its balls specially forced for you in honour of your visit.'

Having all agreed to have jugged hare, the waiter went off to fetch it. Meanwhile Mastosi said in an undertone to me, 'The chef has given a lot of trouble to the hare's balls today and he hopes you and all your guests will be pleased.'

'Come back when we have finished it, and I will then give you a message for the chef,' I replied. By this time the jugged hare had arrived steaming hot on the grill room trolley. When we had all been served I noticed my sister looking at her plate as though looking for something. 'Where are the forced meat balls, I can't find them,' she said. So I sent for Mastosi. 'Where are the "*bals forcés*",' I said, thinking that he would understand me better than if I called them by their proper name. 'Here they are, *mon Genéral*,' and in came a waiter bearing on high a silver dish on which were piled, pyramid shape, a number of big brown balls, each the size of a tennis ball! He gave us each one, saying repeatedly, '*Les bals forcés*, specially made in your honour.' When I say that each forced meat ball was almost larger than the helping of hare, the size of them can be imagined – and they were exceedingly hard!

Afterwards I told the chef personally that the balls should only be about a tenth of the size which he had made them, and that they should be served with the hare and not separately. And this was what he did in future!

16

The Barchester Girls

Most people may have preferred the Grill Room for a quiet meal, but the Cabaret in the Restaurant at the Dorchester was certainly popular in the evening. In 1935 the first lot of American girls – known as Dorchester Girls – had arrived. How precisely R.J.K. was involved with what he called 'Les Girls' is unknown; they were nothing to do with him officially; he was only concerned with attracting private and public functions into the hotel group as a whole. Such a ubiquitous character, however, must have had some sort of connection with them, using the restaurant, as he did, for personal and official entertaining and living, as he did, in the hotel itself. His memoir runs as follows:

'Géneral, si, mais pas un Procureur-Géneral'
It was about this time the first lot of American girls came over from Hollywood and took London by storm – and that they did take London by storm nobody, who was living in London in those days, can deny – and on the evening of the incident I am about to relate, I had asked a woman friend to dine late and see 'our show'.

I say 'our show', because I was then connected with the Dorchester Hotel, having a job which brought me in touch with all the gaiety that is part and parcel of the life of a great Hotel, such as the Dorchester was in those days!

We – my friend and I – had dined and the Cabaret had been on about five minutes or so, the room being packed right out with tables stretching right out into the lounge, so popular and so lovely and attractive were 'Les Girls' as they were called, and whilst watching the 'Show', which was the only 'Show' of its kind in

105

London – in fact one might say outside the States, for to no other country had these lovely American girls come – Sartori came to my table and handed me one of the Cabaret programmes which were on every table, and in which were the photographs of each girl and their names on the different pages. As he did so, he said:

'With his Highness's compliments, General, you will please look at page 9.'

'Which Highness?' I said to Sartori, as there were several Indian Princes, all of them Highnesses, staying at the Dorchester at the time.

'His Highness the Uvarajah of ———, General,' said Sartori, mentioning the name of a well-known Indian Prince, since deceased, and whom I had only met for the first time in the American Bar a few minutes before dinner.

I turned to page 9 on which there were the photographs of five of the girls. At the side of one of them, perhaps the loveliest of them all, whom I knew very well, His Highness had written the words, 'An introduction this evening to this one, please, General! Signed ——— ———.'

Being extremely annoyed that anyone should think that my job in the hotel was to arrange introductions for all and sundry to 'The Dorchester Girls', and especially, as in this case, for a person I hardly knew, I turned over the pages of the booklet, until I came to the last page, which was blank, and on this I wrote:

'*Votre Altesse,*
    "*Je suis un Général, si, mais pas un Procureur-Général.*"

(Sgd.) R. J. Kentish.

General.'

Turning to Sartori, I said: 'Take this to His Highness and give it to him with my compliments, and ask His Highness to turn to the last page.'

'Certainly, General,' said Sartori, and taking it across to where His Highness was sitting, he handed it to him.

I watched him as he turned to the page, which Sartori had pointed out to him, and, as I did so, I saw a look of extreme annoyance come over his face, and then, after he had read what I had written, I saw him pull the page out and tear it into small pieces.

106

That was the last time that particular Highness or any other Highness attempted to make use of me as their 'Procurer'.

* * * * *

But his connection with 'Les Girls' persisted for, at a much later date, he had another experience which he described in a memoir:

'The Barchester Girls'
I was entering the Dorchester Hotel by the main entrance in Park Lane in the small hours of the morning and, as I pushed the revolving door in front of me to pass into the hall, I felt a very heavy push the other way, which nearly knocked me back into the street. Coming out was the bulky form of my friend Valentine Castlerosse. Directly he saw me he said: 'Reggie, you're just the very fellow I want to see. Have you read a book just published called *The Barchester Girls*? It's by John Paddy Carstairs (Nelson Keys' son).'

'No,' I said, 'why?'

'Well, get it at once and read it, because you're libelled on every page, and there's £5,000 damages just sitting waiting for you!!'

'Glory be to God,' I would have said, had I been an Irishman, 'just say it'll be £500 or even £50, and I'll be in your debt for ever! Indade I will!' But, as I was not, I merely said: 'What's the book about?'

'The Dorchester Girls,' said Valentine, 'disguised – very thinly disguised – under the name of "The Barchester Girls", and you're the "Old Colonel", who wants to sleep with each and every one of them every night of the week and the whole year round! Get it at once,' he said, 'and read it, and you've only got to get two people, who know you well, to come into Court – I'll be one of them – and identify you as the "Old Colonel" and there's £5,000 just sitting there waiting for you!!'

'Where can I get the book?'

'Hatchett's in Piccadilly,' he said and with a 'Good night, old boy, give me a ring after you've read it,' he got into a taxi and drove off.

The next morning I started off for Hatchett's, and as I came along Piccadilly I wondered to myself what on earth a well-known restaurant like Hatchett's had to do with books! 'I suppose,' I said to myself, 'young Keys is an habitué of the place and has got the management to let him put the book on sale, or something of that kind.'

Arriving, I walked in and then downstairs, where a head waiter came up and asked if he could do anything for me, etc., etc.

I said: 'I've come to get a book called *The Barchester Girls*.'

'Did you leave it here last night, Sir?' he said, 'Because if so, it will probably be in the Cloakroom.'

'No,' I said, 'I didn't leave it here last night, but I understand it's on sale here. Lord Castlerosse told me so last night.'

'His Lordship must have been mistaken, Sir,' he said, 'we've no books on sale here.'

'No,' I said, 'His Lordship wasn't mistaken. He told me quite distinctly the book was on sale here. Where's your Manager? He may know something about it.'

'I'll get him, Sir,' and off he went, returning in a minute or two with the Manager, to whom I explained the object of my visit.

'Oh,' he said, 'I expect his Lordship meant Hatchards, Sir, the booksellers on the other side of Piccadilly, a few doors down on the right hand side, Sir.'

'Oh, yes, of course,' I said, 'how stupid of me,' and saying, 'I'm very sorry to have bothered you,' I wished him 'Good morning,' and went up the stairs and out into Piccadilly and then across the other side to Hatchard's, the booksellers.

Entering, I inquired for the book, and at the same time I told the fellow – I believe he was the General Manager of the shop – who waited on me, my reason for wishing to get a copy of it at once.

He immediately said he was exceedingly sorry to hear what I had told him, and he added: 'If, after reading it, Sir, you feel that there is anything of a slanderous or libellous nature about you in it, and you will let us know, we will at once communicate with the publishers.'

I told him that, directly I had read the book, I would call again and, with my £5,000 tucked securely under my arm, I departed!

But alas! It was a false alarm – at least I thought so, and so too did two or three of my friends to whom I gave the book to read – for, apart from referring to the 'Old Colonel', who I think the author probably meant to be me, and making one of the girls say to another in their dressing room, when getting ready to go on, 'You'd better watch your step, Helen, otherwise you'll have the old Colonel on to you,' and Helen replying, 'Who cares for "the old

Colonel" anyway? All he wants to do is sleep with one of us every night and then he's happy and so what?' – beyond making one of the girls say that, there was nothing that one could really take exception to, unless one was of the super-sensitive type – and I certainly am not!

As a matter of fact, and to be quite honest, the thought that anyone should think that at my age – I was over 60 at the time – I should desire and apparently be able to perform such a physical feat, gave me a feeling of pride more than anything else! Indeed I regarded it as a compliment and a real feather in my hat!

So a day or two after I rang Valentine up and I said: 'Valentine, my friend, I've read *The Barchester Girls* and I'm taking no action, so we shan't be able to divide that £5,000 after all! Thanks all the same!'

* * * * *

So, leaving the Dorchester Hotel for a while, we must travel up Park Lane to the Banqueting Hall at the Grosvenor House Hotel – not, of course, one of the Gordon Group. Like the Dorchester, this hotel was built after the First World War to compete with the older and, by then, well-established hostelries such as the Ritz, the Savoy and Claridges. The setting for the ensuing anecdote was the monthly luncheon given by Miss Cristina Foyle.

'A Great Russian: Anton Dolin'

The occasion was one of those remarkable luncheons initiated, organized and arranged by Miss Cristina Foyle, a wonderful personality of outstanding ability, universally liked by all and sundry, and famous in the world of books in every country on both sides of the Atlantic.

Each month Cristina organized one of her great – and I use the word 'great' advisedly, for they were in every sense of the word great – luncheons, inviting to be the guests of the Club the leading members of the professions, e.g. Art, Music, Dancing, Writing, Law, Medicine, the Churches, the Services etc., etc., and three or four of the most famous in their own professions being invited to address each gathering.

On the occasion of which I write, the great dancers of the day were the guests of the Club, and amongst the speakers on the toast list was the famous Anton Dolin, the leader of the Russian Ballet. It was just at the moment that the Toast Master was announcing him that the amusing incident I am about to relate occurred.

'My Lady Chairman, My Lords, Ladies and Gentlemen,' thundered out the Toast Master, a wonderful picture of a man in scarlet, 'I pray silence for Monsieur Anton Dolin*, of the Russian Ballet!'

Directly the words 'Anton Dolin' and 'Russian' came out, old Sir Ernest Cochrane, the Dublin soda water magnate, who was sitting next to me, a great Irishman with a terrific brogue, said, so that all around him could hear:

'Anton Dolin be d—d! Anthony Doolan from the County Tipperary, that's his name, and that's where he comes from, and so get the "Russian" and the "Anton Dolin" out of yer moind, Mr Toast Master,' he said.

Much laughter as the great 'Anton Dolin' rose and began his speech, but there wasn't a trace of a brogue about it from start to finish, as there would have been had the great little man hailed, as Sir Ernest said he did, from Tipperary, so I said:

'But what about his brogue, Sir Ernest, if he comes from Tipperary?'

'Holy Jesus!' said Sir Ernest, 'And isn't the man after goin' to school in England for two whole years, learnin' to speak English and tryin' to forget his "Oirish"! Anton Dolin indade! Mr Doolan, that's who yer are; and I'd tache yer not to forgit the Counthry which bore yer, if I had anythin' to do wid yer, Mr Doolan!'

---

* It was commonly reported that he was a Russian and that his name was Antonesky Dolinski, which for stage purposes he had shortened to Anton Dolin. He was, however, an Irishman, his real name being Anthony Doolan and he was born in the County Tipperary.   R.J.K.

17

More Morale

At the beginning of September 1939, Germany attacked Poland. Fulfilling their treaty obligations, Great Britain and France duly declared war on the aggressor nation. As it had done in 1914, the British sent an Expeditionary Force – albeit small and ill-equipped – to France, whose army had manned its Maginot Line, then thought to be impregnable. But Adolf Hitler was so busy invading the Poles that nothing happened in the West until the following May. At home, important buildings, particularly those in London, were shored up by millions of sandbags, whilst the civilian population dug shelters in their back gardens against the expected devastating attack by the German Luftwaffe. Again, nothing happened until the following May. 'All was quiet on the Western Front' during these eight months known as the 'Phoney War'.

Then, on 10 May, the Germans invaded Belgium and, moving southward, successfully outflanked the Maginot Line in a drive towards Paris. The French finally capitulated; the British Army, having advanced into Belgium, was cut off and carried out its famous evacuation to England from the beaches at Dunkirk – minus its equipment. The situation was more than grim.

It must have been very near the time of this débâcle that, apart from Winston Churchill's rallying cry about 'fighting them on the beaches', it was felt something must be done to raise the general morale of a – temporarily at any rate – defenceless nation. To help out, the Dowager Marchioness Townshend of Raynham played her part by organizing – as Chairman – the Officers' Sunday Club at the Dorchester Hotel in London. The Dowager Marchioness had been a very formidable figure during the 1930s during the London Season. She now enlisted Mrs Winston Churchill as President, assisted by the wives of the three Chiefs of Staff, the Ladies Pound, Ironside and Newall, as Vice-Presidents. The Honorary Treasurer was the Hon. Horace Woodhouse. As Honorary Secretary, who indeed could be better than Brigadier General Reggie Kentish, a past expert on the subject of morale?

So, every Sunday, officers both men and women, could bring their friends to an organized *thé-dansant* at the Dorchester Hotel. The Chairman of the Entertainment Committee was the well-known impresario, Mr Charles Cochrane, for during or after the drinking of tea there was a Cabaret. The band was really Ambrose's, all now in the RAF but re-assembled as a single unit for the occasion, and all, like the officers, presumably at a loose end.

An excellent account of what went on at these morale raising functions is provided from an extract from an article called 'The Social Round-About', which was written by Bridget Chetwynd and appeared in a glossy magazine on 16 October 1940:

Officers' Sunday Club
Here youth and beauty are to be found, transforming the English Sunday into a gay affair. The basic ingredients of hunt balls, the Berkeley, Ascot and the Highland Games, have, in wartime, boiled themselves down to this. Mothers, proud or petulant, lead around daughters gay or sulky, while the inevitable spanking blondes hold the floor with the lads in khaki, kilts and Air Force blue.

It all happens at the Dorchester, on tea and dainty sandwiches, and is organized by Lady Townshend, who did the same thing in the last war. The object is to prevent our brave boys in the officer category from being at a loose end during the above-mentioned grim institution, the English Sunday, and the flower of our girlhood is there to help.

General Kentish is honorary secretary, and is there throughout, behaving rather like a Field Master during an unwieldy day with the Quorn, and making some pretty good jokes on the side. I am told that among his other functions are speeches on morale: during the Dutch, Belgian, and French 'debacles' he was, like everyone else, usually a lap behind, but undeterred. I would back him to create morale by thin air out of disaster.

* * * * *

Bridget Chetwynd went on to say that 9,256 had attended the first 16 gatherings, and then proceeded to note those people of interest on this particular Sunday. She was writing, of course, for that pictorially glossy magazine, the *Tatler*, which used to record the social doings of those belonging to a leisured class.

But all good things must come to an end. The Field Master had always disliked committees, especially those which cramped his style, and, in due course, he found the formidable Dowager Marchioness and her lady supporters more than he could take. At some date, he resigned. This impetuous and restless man had always jumped from one thing to another, and his next enthusiastic venture was already in the pipeline. From the beginning of the War onward he had pestered the War Office with countless letters; he was finally given permission to put on the defunct uniform of a Brigadier General – at the age of 64 – in order to lecture to the Officer Cadet Training Units (OCTUs) and other Establishments on 'Leadership and Morale', his speciality during the First World War.

After our ignominious but very successful exit from France via Dunkirk, it was expected that, despite the inimitable oratory of Winston Churchill (and the efforts of the Dowager Marchioness on Sunday afternoons!), that our morale was found to be at a low ebb. The ill-equipped remnants of the Army were positioned along the eastern and southern coastlines of England to try to stave off the expected German invasion. Our pitifully small number of fighter aircraft were lying inland, ready to take on the German Luftwaffe. It was the Spitfire and Hurricane pilots who saved the day for us – known as the Battle of Britain – by creating havoc amongst the enemy bombers and their fighter escorts which crossed the coastline as a preliminary to the planned invasion by sea. The successful outcome of this air battle made Hitler change his mind, thus giving us a prolonged period in which to rearm ourselves.

113

The virtual second line of defence was the Home Guard (Dad's Army), officially raised in May 1940, which consisted of the very young and the very old (65 was the upper limit). Its duties were, in the early days, to observe and report; its armament comprised, *inter alia*, sporting shotguns and home-made Molotov cocktail bombs. The first clothing issued was a slovenly looking denim suit with private headgear to taste; the most popular in order of merit being a (a) homburg or trilby, (b) porkpie, (c) cloth cap, (d) choice of moleskin caps, straw boaters, berets or deerstalkers.

The general unpreparedness for war in 1939 had shocked R.J.K. Perhaps the final straw which lowered his own morale to rock bottom was the issue of pikes to the Home Guard to supplement the 12-bore shotguns and scanty issue of rifles. One of his unpublished memoirs described a meeting in Bournemouth addressed by Lord Croft, Under-Secretary of State for War, for which constituency he had been the MP for 25 years, as Sir Henry Page Croft. He called it '*Ora Pro Nobis*'. Lord Croft ended his talk as follows:

'And now, ladies and gentlemen [N.B. his Lordship's audience was mostly composed of the elderly and aged], I have kept to the end something, which I feel sure will cheer you all up and enable you to retire to your beds at night with a feeling of complete confidence in our Home Defences and in the ability of the gallant men who are manning them to keep the hated enemy from our shores. WE HAVE DECIDED TO ARM – IN FACT THE ARMING HAS ACTUALLY BEGUN – THE HOME GUARD WITH PIKES!'

Immediately there broke out from all parts of the hall cheers, clapping of hands and cries of 'Good old Croft', 'He's done it again', 'God bless you my Lord' and so on, during which his Lordship, picking up his walking stick, which was lying with his hat on the table in front of him, and using it as though it had been a pike and handling it with great dexterity, made several vigorous and vicious lunges at the Chairman, Alderman Bigbody, a big and and corpulent gentleman, as his name denotes, who had considerable difficulty in avoiding the onslaught. Finally, his Lordship, perspiring freely, replaced his 'pike' on the table, and the Chairman, thankful he had escaped serious injury, and, fearful lest his Lordship might start again, hurriedly proposed a very hearty vote of thanks to the speaker and brought the meeting to a close.

The *Daily Mail* published a report of the meeting, headed 'Lord Croft arms the Home Guard with Pikes' which included a poem:

'Epitaph to a Very Brave Man'
'Ora Pro Nobis'
Here Lies a victim of the Huns!
He had a pike but they had guns!!
And now, he wonders, gone aloft!!!
Whether to curse the Huns or Croft!!!!
'Bee'

Of the '100 Memoirs' which he left for posterity, this is the only one which is 'suspect', for R.J.K. was neither present in Bournemouth nor had he any personal connection with it. The wording of the story is not only cynical but improbable! It was possibly an attempt, when written in 1943, to express his sadness and contempt for the parlous defence situation prevailing in 1940 and before. The thought of the Home Guard, arrayed with ill-fitting denims, protected by trilby hats and carrying pikes, going forth to confront the German Panzer Divisions in our countryside, had not been a very welcome or inspiring thought.

R.J.K. was most persistent on the telephone and on paper. Even so, it was one of the wonders of two World Wars that the War Office (now part of the Ministry of Defence) allowed a 64-year-old Brigadier General to don the extinct uniform of a rank which had been abolished after the First World War to lecture on 'Leadership, Morale and *Esprit de Corps*' to budding officers and others. It was an intermittent assignment. Did he receive the pay of a modern Brigadier, or was he given a fixed sum and travelling expenses on each occasion? The talks were given primarily to the many OCTUs but occasionally to static army units, the Home Guard, RAF stations, and to a few ships. If morale was apt to be lacking in 1940, he certainly seems to have enhanced it, if only temporarily, during his talks up to the end of 1942.

From: Anonymous person
         Army & Navy Club
         Pall Mall, SW1

My son said you lectured at Aldershot last week on 'Leadership'. Those who heard you unanimously agreed it was 'All Balls' from start to finish and were bored stiff.

They want to get on with their practical training, not listen to rubbish from old men who are useless gasbags. Knowing you . . . I concur.'

Signed: Brother Anno Domini

This was doubtless a figment of his own imagination, constantly used as that successful opening gambit which every good lecturer should have: something which is amusing to make people sit up and listen thereafter. But he really had no need for gadgets of this sort; he knew how to hold an audience. Out of eight OCTUs he visited all asked him to come again when there was a new intake of cadets.

From 124 OCTU:
Thank you very much for the four lectures you gave. I am afraid it was rather a lot to ask from you, but I am sure the cadets enjoyed every minute of it, and you gave them many good laughs. Just what they wanted. I will let you know when we should like you to come again.

From 151 OCTU:
I am glad to hear you enjoyed your visit to Mons Barracks. I can assure you we all enjoyed listening to your words of wisdom. I am quite convinced that talks of this description do an immense amount of good. I hope you will come and see us again, and I shall always be ready to gather the lads together for you.

From Chief Welfare Officer, Southern Command:
I am very glad indeed I came over to Camberley from Salisbury to hear you talk to the cadets yesterday. It was worth it; my adopted son tells me it was far and away the best outside lecture they have had. You ought to go all over the country.

From a lady friend:
My brother heard you lecture at Llandrindod Wells. He wrote and told us that you were splendid and worth more than the whole of the ENSA concerts put together.

ENSA was the organization which provided entertainment for the Forces, both at home and overseas. R.J.K. could not resist sending this last one to Basil Dean, Head of ENSA, who, like Queen Victoria, was NOT amused! He claims to have addressed 100,000 all told and at the end of 1942 he decided that this was enough, discarding the uniform to go and live at the Three Swans Hotel in Hungerford, Berks, until the end of the War.

INTERLUDES IN DEVON

An Incident in Devon

by R.J.K., called 'Wonderful Devonians'

SCENE: TIME: PLACE: The Parcels Office, Kingsbridge, South Devon, two or three days before Christmas 1941. *DRAMATIS PERSONAE*: Edgar, the old Head Porter, who's been at Kingsbridge for years; Mick his colleague; a couple of young Airmen; a woman of uncertain age, poor but respectable – and myself.

* * * * *

I was staying at Salcombe at the time, and I had occasion to go into Kingsbridge to see if a parcel I was expecting from Oxford had arrived. As I entered the Parcels Office I was greeted by Edgar with a:

'Good marnin', Mr Kentish.'

'I'm not a "Mr",' I said, 'I'm a General!'

'Oh, sorry Colonel,' said Edgar.

'Damn it, man, I said "General", not "Colonel".'

I think he was just going to say 'Sorry, Mr Kentish, I meant General,' when in came Mick, the other porter, who knew me, having seen me at the station on many occasions.

'Good marnin',', Major!' he said as he passed me.

'Well, I'm damned,' I said, 'I've just this moment, and after a hell of an effort, got up from "Mr" to "General", and now you come and put me back to "Major". 'Isn't it the limit?' I said, turning to the two young Airmen.

118

'Sorry, Captain!' said Mick.

Well, that finished it, and all the two young Airmen, the middle-aged respectable woman, Edgar and self could do was just to burst out laughing, and then, giving Edgar and Mick each a Christmas Box and, wishing them both a very happy Xmas, I departed!

Another Incident in Devon

by R.J.K., called 'Why We're Now Absolutely Certain to Lose the War'

SCENE: TIME: PLACE: The Ferry Inn, Salcombe, South Devon, sometime in January. 1942.
DRAMATIS PERSONAE: Two elderly gentlemen together in the Inn just before lunch – and myself, knowing neither but within earshot of their conversation.

* * * * *

'Have you heard the latest?' said the first elderly old gentleman.

'No,' said the other. 'I've not listened in or seen a paper yet. Is it good or bad?'

'D—d bad,' said the first. 'I got a letter from my laundry this morning, telling me that owing to war difficulties they regretted that in future they would not be able to starch my collars! Pretty serious, don't you think?'

'Yes,' said the other. 'What are you going to do about it?'

'Oh, just make the best of it I suppose, and wear 'em without starch! What would you do?'

'The same,' said the other, 'in fact it's the only thing you can do! Heard any more news?'

'Nothing of importance, except the sinking of the *Prince of Wales* and the *Repulse* but, in consequence of that and on the motion of Councillor Pritchard, I hear that the Salcombe Council is going to re-continue salving their scrap metal – you know they discontinued salving it three or four weeks ago because the Minister of Supply wouldn't or couldn't

119

make arrangements to collect it – and so we ought to soon have enough to build a couple more ships to take their place!'

'Good,' said the other. 'Let's have a drink on it!'

'Two doubles, Fred, please,' and then: 'Well! here's to Councillor Pritchard!'

'To Councillor Pritchard,' said the other.

'God bless him!' murmured both, and 'Wonderful Salcombe' murmured I to myself, and 'having one' too, I hied me back to my hotel to lunch!

18

'This Detestable, Foul and Filthy Thing called War'

By 1943 R.J.K., now aged 67, had gone to live at the Three Swans Hotel, Hungerford, Berkshire, where he remained, off and on, for the duration of the war. The outcome of this long drawn-out struggle was now more cheerful: an eventual victory of the Allies.

R.J.K. was aggrieved that so many of 'his' playing fields had been ploughed up or used as military encampments in aid of the war effort. Would they ever come back to life? How sad that one of his own personal achievements had come to this, but a far worse thing was the enormity of the horror that had overtaken the world.

He had always been astounded that England had entered the war in 1939 so thoroughly ill-equipped to fight. The First World War had been bad enough, but this current war was far worse. By 1945 there were to be over 50 million dead and a far greater number injured, some permanently. Six million Jews were to meet their death in the Nazi gas chambers; millions of people were 'displaced' as foreign workers in Europe and Asia; whole towns and cities were to be razed to the ground by intensive bombing. Even if 'his' playing fields were brought back to life, would an even worse conflagration break out in 20 or 30 years' time, which would end civilization the world over?

With nothing much to occupy him in Hungerford, and a probable shortage of good cheer in the hotel bar, his mind began to function; he churned out ream after ream of his pencilled 'scribble', which some unfortunate typist – who had obviously not been called up for war work – had to decipher and punctuate.

The famous writer, H.G. Wells, who had predicted the atom

121

bomb in 1918 and terrorism in his book *The World Set Free* (1914), had also written in *War and the Future* (1917) the following:

> There is an enormous mass of people who – in spite of the fact that their minds are concentrated on the various aspects of this war – are neither doing or trying to do anything about it at all. It may, for anything they have learnt about it, happen to them again. I think, though, that this war may start a process of thought which will arrest or prevent another great catastrophe.

That was in 1917, but it gave R.J.K. the idea that people in the present war must start to think about its aftermath. He himself, therefore, would collect the ideas of men and women well-known in public life and publish them in a book; ideas which would make other people start to think as well. So he wrote a personal letter – each one different – on two pages of quarto-size paper to 80 people, distinguished in their own line of country, asking them to contribute to his proposed book. This was accompanied by a questionnaire, and he asked that replies to it should not exceed three or four thousand words. In general, the questionnaire asked: (a) Could this war have been prevented? (b) Who are the people who took us into the war almost totally unprepared? and (c) What steps can be taken and by whom to avoid a more terrible war in 20 or 30 years' time? All sorts of men and women were written to: politicians, journalists, industrialists, churchmen, Quakers, atheists, service chiefs and academics.

About 30 of these sent a contribution, and permission was given by Winston Churchill and H.G. Wells to quote extracts from some of their previous writings. Of the 50 who did not wish to commit themselves in writing, most pleaded pressure of work in other directions. Some, though, thought that a higgledy-piggledy assortments of views was worthless without a final conclusion or summing up; others objected to having their names linked with pacifists. One person was quite blunt: 'There have been wars since the beginning of time, there will be wars until the end of time, so why waste words on trying to stop them.'

In 1943, after vigorous efforts to persuade unwilling participants to be included, R.J.K. assembled his proposed book. It was to include his own foreword and the final 30 people who were willing to take part in this inquiry. It was to be called *Salvation or Damnation* and it ran into about 100,000 words. No one would profit from its publication except a named military charity. His old friend Major General J.F.C. (Boney) Fuller, military critic and author of over 30 books, gave skilled advice. 'Boney' Fuller, whom R.J.K. had known for most of his life, vetted each contribution and gave his opinion on the layout of the finished article. He was 'certain that the book would be published', but it never was. There is no evidence that it ever found its way to a publisher. The typescript was found in a suitcase after my uncle's death in 1956 and has lain in my attic, gathering dust, until now.

One of his critics had written: 'Who can possibly foresee what post-war conditions will be? You are wasting your time.' It is hardly surprising that the contributors, writing in 1943, failed to take into account developments which were of crucial importance in the formation of the post-war world: the atom bomb, the power struggle between capitalism and communism, the 'Iron Curtain', the 'Cold War'; conditions which were to prevail for the next 45 years. Several collaborators in the never-published book suggested that the world should be divided into spheres, with wartime allies, the USA, Great Britain, Russia and China, keeping the peace by controlling armaments, economies and trade in their respective areas. They appear not have foreseen that the wartime allies would no longer be allies in a world divided between capitalism and communism, or that the British Empire would be dissolved by 1960 and that Britain would no longer be a world power. The United Nations Organization has done sterling work in many directions, but can it stop wars? Conflicts since the Cold War have shown up its weaknesses.

Perhaps the most encouraging sign for the above contributors would be the growth of the European Union: a body with its own parliament, free trade and, possibly, a single currency in the near future. It means, of course, that its constituent states must forego a small measure of sovereignty, but that is something recommended by several of R.J.K.'s collaborators.

My uncle's Foreword to the proposed book was slightly

bombastic and Churchillian. It contained the following passages:

Twenty-nine years ago, i.e. in 1914, the British Empire became involved in a life and death struggle for its existence with Germany. For four very bloody years the flower of the youth of our Country and our Dominions fought and nearly bled itself to death. The crosses on the graves of over a million of our young men, who sacrificed their lives on the battlefield, give poignant proof of what I say.

At the outbreak of the struggle England was found completely unprepared – save for the Navy, at the head of which by an act of God happened to be Winston Churchill and, which before the war had actually been declared, had, by another act of God, been mobilized for manoeuvres in Home waters. With an Army composed of half a dozen highly trained but badly equipped Regular divisions, fourteen almost completely untrained and far worse equipped Territorial divisions and a handful of aeroplanes, she went to war against the greatest military machine the world, up to then, had ever seen, viz. the mighty German Army under its Warlord, the Emperor William II.

Somehow by a miracle, which the more devout and religious minded declared must have been heaven sent, our very gallant Regular Army – the 'Old Contemptibles' – with the help of a dozen or so equally gallant regiments of the Territorial Army, succeeded in holding the German hosts until such time as Lord Kitchener had raised, trained and sent to France the divisions of his New Army. Then, side by side with our allies, and later with the Americans, we fought and eventually, with the aid of our Navy, broke the hearts of the German people and then of the German Army and Navy. We finally emerged triumphant.

The war over, our people, nauseated with and sick of the whole ghastly business, immediately sheathed and threw aside their swords, turning to their pre-war peacetime pursuits and occupations; not one single soul raising his or her voice at the terrible slaughter the war had occasioned or seeking shoulders on which to place the responsibility either for the war itself or for the complete state of unpreparedness which England was in when war was declared. Nobody showed the slightest concern about these vitally important matters. As I have already said, everyone turned to their pre-war pursuits and occupations, each trying to forget the war and all to do with it. It was quite obvious, though, that in the face of

124

such a colossal tragedy – which had cost us over a million killed and thousands blinded and maimed for life – a searching inquiry should have been held into the causes which had brought the war about; fixing responsibility and recommending steps to be taken to prevent such a tragedy befalling us again.

But no such inquiry took place. Save for standing bare-headed for a few minutes on Armistice Sunday and collecting three or four hundred thousand pounds every year for the British Legion, the nation soon forgot its million dead. It was apparently quite unmindful of the thousands and thousands of ex-servicemen who were unable to find work, and of the misery all this unemployment had brought into the homes of her people. England sank back into the same old blissful state of oblivion which she had sunk into after the South African War; leaving things as she had left them then, i.e. to the politicians, although everyone knew, or should have known, that to no more untrustworthy body of men could the country's affairs and interests have been entrusted.

Then in 1939 came the awakening. And a very rude awakening it was too for, before she knew where she was, England found herself at war again and – *mirabile dictu* – with the very enemy she had worsted and beaten to its knees only a mere twenty years before. Unbelievable as it may seem, we were even more unprepared for war than in 1914.

At the time everyone was so overwhelmed with the appalling – and I use this word advisedly – situation which confronted us and so great was the blow when it fell and so grave the danger that threatened us all, that no one had the time to sit down and think it all out. The one thought uppermost in the minds of every man, woman and child in the islands was how to keep the German hordes from invading and completely destroying our country. With that as our main objective and under the inspiration of a great leader, of whom historians in days to come will surely say 'he was the greatest Englishman of all time', the whole nation 'turned to', and putting forth its greatest effort, fought back foot by foot with the result that, today, victory, if not yet with us, is at any rate well in sight.

The great mass of the population had not time to sit down and think it all out. For this reason, no clear and concerted demand came from the people claiming as a right to know why this second and even more terrible catastrophe had come upon them so soon after the first, which in all conscience was terrible enough. This did not mean, however, that the people were not concerned or interested in the matter, or all they desired was to win the war first and then settle down again to enjoy a life of peace, ease and plenty.

On the contrary, there were many who, like myself, though past the age for war work but not past the age for thinking, did find time to sit down and think it out. As a result, we came to the conclusion quite definitely that some one must have blundered – and blundered grievously – to have allowed such a catastrophe to have come upon us again.

As I write these lines today at the end of 1943, the whole situation has changed; the war has veered round definitely in favour of the Allies to such an extent that Mussolini, one of the two super-gangsters, has been deposed by his own people. His soldiers, sailors and airmen have surrendered and are now fighting with us. He himself, a fugitive from justice, is sheltering in some mountain fortress in the north of Italy under the wing of Hitler, whose own downfall is also only a question of time.

This being the case, the planning of the post-war world has become a matter of primary and outstanding importance. Unless, first of all, a plan is found whereby the peace of the world can be maintained, all other plans and schemes of a social and economic nature are just wastes of time, energy and brain power. My view is, I know, shared by thousands of my fellow countrymen and women that the causes which brought this war about, so far as our leaders are concerned, most certainly should be inquired into. Lastly, I am of the opinion that it is the duty of everyone who is not engaged in war work, who has the time, to be thinking of these problems. I have decided to make my own contribution to the great post-war plan in the form of this book, in which will be found not only my own views on these matters but also those of a number of people, some of distinction and others not so distinguished or well-known, but all possessing common sense and who are patriots to their finger tips.

It seems to me that the simplest way of ascertaining what people are thinking about these matters would be to ask them straight away what their views were. So I sent a questionnaire to 80 well-known people. 30 of these have sent me their answers.

The Questionnaire

1. (a) Are you of the opinion that this war might have been prevented?

    and, if so,

    (b) How and by what means?

    and

    (c) So far as England is concerned, who are the people in this country who you hold responsible for not having taken the said means?

2. England was in even greater state of unpreparedness for war against Germany in 1939 than she was in 1914 (*vide* General Viscount Gort's *Despatches* written after Dunkirk). Whom do you hold responsible for this?

3. (a) Are you of the opinion that the responsible persons referred in Question 1 (c) and 2 should be brought to trial?

    and, if so,

    (b) How and by what means, bearing in mind that the procedure, whereby in the olden days, men holding high office were impeached in and by the House of Commons and brought to trial in and by the House of Lords, no longer obtains.

4. Having regard to the fact that for the second time within the memory of the greater part of the population this world tragedy has come upon us, and that, unless certain steps are taken, another war, even more terrible in its effect, will most assuredly break out in, say 1960 or 1970, what steps do you suggest should be taken and by whom and when, to prevent such another world disaster?

The opening chapter of the proposed book was to have been H.G. Wells's extracts from his *War and the Future* and an article in the *Sunday Express* (1941) called 'How Can This War End?'

Dear Mr. Wells,
　　　　My friends tell me it would be a waste of time to ask the big men of letters to answer my questions. I have ignored their advice because I hold to the opinion that, regarding this detestable, foul and filthy thing called war, no one who has practical ideas of how to prevent it can or dare or has the right to keep them to himself.

Yours sincerely,

R.J.K.

His wife, writing from Hanover Terrace, Regents Park, NW1 on 7 June 1943, said, 'Mr H.G. Wells is very pleased for you to use his two articles — But as he makes an iron rule against giving something for nothing, he would stipulate that you should send a contribution of at least 10/6d to the Diabetic Association, of which he is President.'

The *Daily Express* article began by extolling the eight articles of the Atlantic Charter signed by Churchill and Roosevelt in August 1941, which stressed, *inter alia*, that they would 'further the enjoyment of all States of access on equal terms to the trade and materials of the world.' This was to be the theme adopted by several of R.J.K.'s contributors, as was the suggestion by H.G. Wells that every state must relinquish absolute sovereignty as far as world-wide federal needs are concerned. 'A gigantic prospect,' was H.G. Wells's comment!

The second chapter of the proposed book was provided, with his permission, by the then Prime Minister, Winston Churchill. It was made up of extracts from his book *Step by Step* based on fortnightly letters he had written on Foreign Policy and Defence between 1936 and 1939. By the former year Germany had broken both the Treaty of Versailles (1919) and the Locarno Pact (1925); she had adopted a policy of re-armament in 1935 and had marched into and re-militarized the Rhineland in early 1936. Unlike other Western statesmen, he had seen that the rapid re-armament of Germany since the advent of Adolf Hitler would inevitably lead to another war – unless! In these fortnightly letters he had issued – in his superb and inimitable prose – the clarion call 'Stop it Now', which was unheeded until it was too late.

Churchill produced figures to prove that Germany was increasing her arms expenditure by billions of marks; all leading and working up to war. There are four or five million active, intelligent, valiant Germans, he wrote, working night and day. What is it all for? Certainly it is not for fun: something quite extraordinary is afoot. All the signals are at danger. The red lights flash through the gloom. Let peaceful folk beware. It is time to pay attention and to be well prepared.

The modern world, he went on, presents an extraordinary spectacle of almost everybody wishing to prevent or avoid war, and yet it is coming remorselessly nearer to almost everybody. Surely this will be the great mystery which future generations will find among the records and, perhaps, the ruins of our age. How was it, historians will ask, that these vast, fairly intelligent, educated communities were so helpless and futile as to allow themselves to become victims of their own processes and of what they most abhorred? The answer will be, 'They had no plan'.

Churchill was intimating that all was not well with the statesmen and people of the world. It was something that also struck R.J.K. in 1943; something which prompted him to try to discover from 80 intelligent people what they were thinking about it all after the disaster had occurred in 1939 – and how such a similar situation could be avoided in the future.

19

'Salvation or Damnation'

The distinguished and intelligent people who submitted a total of nearly 90,000 words for the proposed book were – apart from hoping to subscribe to a military charity – laying themselves open to a charge of 'obstructing the war effort'. R.J.K.'s friend and arch-collaborator, Major General 'Boney' Fuller, had written to him in February 1943, 'I cannot help feeling that if we let ourselves go full out we shall see the inside of Brixton Prison.' And again in the following May, 'Herewith my last obituary notice. It will come in handy when I am shot for having written for you what I have.'

Question 1 **Could the Second World War have been prevented?**

The longest contribution came from 'Boney' himself. What was the basic cause of this war, he asked. The seeds were sown in 1919 at Versailles, he continued. After a compassionate gesture of kindness by Winston Churchill and a statement by Lloyd George that there must be no sense of revenge, the Allies dictated a Peace Treaty which showed exactly that. The hate propaganda of the preceding four years, fanned by the Press – particularly by the Northcliffe group – had won the day. Germany was to be almost totally disarmed, the Rhineland was to be demilitarized and occupied by the Allies (this only lasted until 1930), and she was to pay 132 million gold marks (reduced in later years) in reparation. This, asserted Fuller, resulted in a subsequent crippling inflation and unemployment which eventually produced Adolf Hitler, who put the 6 million workless into a new conscript army or into munition factories, all in defiance of clauses in the Versailles Peace Treaty of 1919. Thus were sown the seeds of a new war.

This view was taken by others, including General Sir Hubert Gough, who had commanded the 5th Army in France in 1916, the Army which had had under its command the Cavalry Divisions which were to carry out the pursuit of the Germans after the initial breakthrough in the Somme. He was convinced that the Allies should have occupied the large German towns in 1918 for a period of at least 10 years, at the same time rebuilding the economy, and thus avoiding the emergence of the Austrian house decorator and ex-army corporal, Adolf Hitler. (This was what in effect happened after the German surrender in 1945, in the form of Military Government of Enemy Territories.)

Another seed sown in 1919, which sprouted wrongly, was the emergence of the League of Nations, conceived by the American President, Woodrow Wilson. Unfortunately, America chose not to join in, Russia was not asked to, and none of our wartime enemies were allowed to. Many countries subsequently sheltered under it; a caucus which in fact had no teeth and proved unable – not even by sanctions – to avert any sort of war. This was the view of most of R.J.K.'s contributors.

The seeds of a future war having been sown in 1919, could the Second World War have been averted? Here we have the opinion of Lord Davies, former Liberal MP, Parliamentary Secretary to Lloyd George (1916/17), Vice President of the British League of Nations Union and founder of the New Commonwealth Society for the establishment of an International Equity Tribunal and International Police Force.

A few years after the Versailles Treaty, the British and French Governments could have called a New Peace Conference. Here victors and vanquished, in a calmer and less tense atmosphere, could have discussed and negotiated a revision of the 1919 Treaty. It might have been possible that the grievances – real or imaginary – could have been disposed of by mutual consent or arbitration.

Then Germany would have been invited to join the League of Nations.

Unfortunately this Conference was never held. Hitler came to power and eventually repudiated clauses in the Versailles Treaty by unilateral acts, whilst the Allied Governments contented themselves with futile protests, taking no steps to ensure that the public law was upheld.

Another contributor, who thought the war could have been averted, was the Duke of Bedford, a member of the Peace Pledge Union and a leading Christian Pacifist; one, in fact, whom several others did not wish to be seen in print with! His thoughts were that, after taking the initiative in securing an early remedy to the injustices of the Versailles Treaty, we should have seen that the world's resources were available to everyone who needed them; this would have kept people happy, for the cause of wars is always a search for food.

This was the view also – amongst many others – of Lieutenant Colonel Clive Garsia, a distinguished soldier of the First World War and the author of three books: *Tenacity* (1927), *A Key to Victory, a Study in War Planning* (1940), and *Planning the War* (1941). He wrote:

Could this present war have been prevented? Yes, provided (and the proviso then makes Yes tantamount to No) that the Allies:

(a)   had occupied Berlin in 1919
(b)   Germany had been completely disarmed
(c)   Britain and France had stood shoulder to shoulder in making the League of Nations a true bulwark of peace
(d)   Britain and France had taken immediate action in the face of unilateral violations by Germany of the Versailles Treaty
(e)   the problem of world trade had been tackled on a world basis.

World peace can be achieved by a system of planning, centrally directed, which controls the primary elements of world trade, i.e. for instance, wheat, oil, rubber, cotton, machinery, electrical equipment and capital movements.

Another contributor, anonymously described as a 'Man of much learning: Dr H. St L.K.', was equally pessimistic:

> I cannot see anything practicable that could have stopped the arrogance of Germany from going into the ordeal of battle. The only thing that might have done so – an impossible thing – was:
>
> (a)   The British Empire, the USA and the USSR should have leaguered themselves together in 1935,
> and
> (b)   They should each and all three have militarized themselves from then onwards
>
> This, of course, is what has now happened (1943). I do not see how it could have happened before.

Question 2   'Who was responsible in England for not having prevented the war and for sending us into it quite unprepared?'

It would seem that war might have been prevented if certain commitments had been carried out collectively by the former wartime Allies, i.e. maintaining strong enough military forces to enable the League of Nations to become a real bulwark for peace and/or to take immediate action in the face of unilateral action by Germany and, subsequently, by Italy and Japan. But these commitments were not carried out either individually or collectively, and so the world drifted into a conflict in 1939 which was to cause 60 million deaths.

If collective responsibility or action was absent, who, in England, failed to play a part in doing what should have been done? Here the seeker after truth, R.J.K., was looking for someone's blood and, as will be seen in the Epilogue, he was successful. For him honour was satisfied, even though the results of his inquiry were never published. Many of his contributors blamed the people of this country as a whole. Surely they had elected the various governments – but two in particular exonerated them.

The first was R.J.K.'s friend, 'Boney' Fuller:

From the formation of the League of Nations onwards, from plat-form and pulpit, from rostrum and soapbox, a sloppy, sentimental and utterly fraudulent pacifism was drummed into the ears of the people. War was exorcized, war was anathematized, war was even outlawed! The Army was reduced to its pre-war footing; the Navy was allowed to fall into ruin; the RAF was all but strangled. Even Cadet Corps were abolished; even Territorial soldiers were prohib-ited from drilling in the London Parks.

The second was Major General H. Rowan Robertson, a distin-guished soldier, the author of many publications concerning Imperial Defence and a persistent advocate up to 1943 of a Ministry of Defence. He berated the 'intellectuals' for turning the population into a state of inertia and, to quote from the words of Douglas Reed in his best-selling book *Insanity Fair* – which had run into 18 reprints in 1938 – into a state of ostrichism.

The Intellectuals were dangerous. In the decades that led up to 1939, they continuously taught our youth to despise religion, loyalty, patriotism and courage. They never tired of heaping calumny and ridicule on the fighting forces. They preached paci-fism, they created a general distaste for military service and they hampered the Ministers of War in their endeavours to place the defences of the country on a sound footing .... They still have a public which admires their nimble art in the arenas opened to them by the BBC and the columns of our Press.

If, rightly or wrongly, the British public are exonerated, then the blame must surely lie with the Government and politicians. The thoughts of Frank Owen were mirrored in a succinct and lucid offering of some 3,000 words. Owen had been the editor of the *Evening Standard* until 1943, but at the time of writing what he did write, he was a trooper in the Royal Armoured Corps! One of his themes:

This country is said to be a democracy; millions of people in arms in 1943 believe that proposition and are in arms defending it against the totalitarian States of Germany and Italy. Although no political party placed the security of the country first in their election programme, it is surely an understood thing that this is,

134

and ever must be, the prime and basic consideration of any Government. Of course people expect their rulers to discharge this elementary duty. These leaders, however, led the nation – almost unarmed by comparison with totalitarian standards – into war against the most formidable machine in the whole history of the world. They bungled the peace so that after two brief campaigns in Norway and France the British Army could muster rifles enough for one and a half Divisions, whilst available tanks numbered 50. Against this pitiable equipment the enemy marshalled 180 Divisions, with possibly between 6,000 and 10,000 tanks ...

I consider that General Kentish does his country a notable service by demanding that the men who misled us shall be exposed by a public enquiry. After all, those who aspire to rule their fellow men may reasonably be expected to have a fuller knowledge of public affairs than the ordinary citizen; even politicians arriving in office abysmally ignorant at once gain access to all sorts of special confidential information.

So who were the guilty men? The most frequently mentioned were – apart from Ramsay MacDonald, Leader of the Labour Party and a renowned pacifist – all the office holders in the Conservative Party, which, with the exception of two brief periods, was the dominant party in government between the two World Wars. The Tory Prime Minister, Stanley Baldwin, came out of it worst:

Supposing I had gone to the country and said that Germany was re-arming and that we must re-arm, does anybody think that this pacifist democracy would have rallied to the cry at that moment? I cannot think of anything that would have made the loss of the election from my point of view more certain.

These are the classic words of Stanley Baldwin. Rather than let the Labour Party into office, he had preferred to keep the people in ignorance of our weak state and, furthermore, done nothing – or very little about it – afterwards.

Statesmen can be encouraged to tell the people the truth, and Winston Churchill has achieved glory for doing fearlessly just that, but Baldwin's name is liable to stink in the nostrils of posterity for his cowardice at a time when the crisis might still have been averted. That a Prime Minister should have lied to the electorate in order to win an election is altogether over the odds.

(Lieutenant Colonel Clive Garsia)

Major General H. Rowan Robinson produced these two indictments:

(a) Sir Samuel Hoare was long in office as Air Minister during the years in which the RAF was allowed to slip to fifth place among the Air Forces of the world.

(b) Sir Thomas Inskip in 1936 was appointed by Mr Baldwin to be Minister for the Co-ordination of Defence, in spite of his incredible lack of capacity for that task. Here are some of the mistakes he made. Early in 1936 he assured a group of journalists that only those ignorant of the true position could feel any uneasiness about the British re-armament programme. 'There is in almost everything – I think I may say everything – a flood of armaments and equipment which we need to complete our defence.' 'Britain possesses the best of all anti-aircraft defences in the world.'

This was the man, adds Rowan Robinson, who was jointly responsible with Mr Hore-Belisha for sending our army to France in 1939 without a single Armoured Division.

Mrs E.O. Lorimer was another who comprehensively listed the guilty men. In 1943 she was a Tutor in German Philology at Somerville College, Oxford. Hitler's sudden rape of Austria in 1938 had roused her to a realization that the Brownshirt 'tub thumper' was not a man of straw but was setting out to fulfil the manic programme contained in his book *Mein Kampf*. Her indictment runs as follows:

Again, the true state of affairs was deliberately concealed from the British public by lying or misleading statements made in the House by Ministers whom we were entitled to believe we could trust. Our defences remained totally inadequate while ministers unashamedly boasted of our strength . . . .

Then followed the shame of Munich. Among the guilty are: in the foreground, Stanley Baldwin, John Simon, Frederick

136

Henry Maugham, Thomas Inskip, Neville Chamberlain, Nevile Henderson, Walter Runciman and the entire Cabinet personnel, with Horace Wilson, Henry David Reginald Margesson and doubtless many others in the background. The alarming aspect of the situation is that, far from having been publicly censured or discredited, most of those men still enjoy titles and high office in Britain today and exert influence in our public life.

Stanley Baldwin is still Earl Baldwin of Bewdley (created in 1937) and a member of His Majesty's Privy Council.

John Simon was created Viscount in 1940 and is now Lord High Chancellor of England, Speaker of the House of Lords and a Privy Councillor.

Frederick Herbert Maugham (ex-Lord High Chancellor) was created Viscount in 1939 and is a Privy Councillor.

Thomas Inskip, camouflaged as Viscount Caldecote (created 1939), is now Lord Chief Justice of England and a Privy Councillor.

Neville Chamberlain has gone to his account. May he rest in peace if he can.

Nevile Henderson is a GCMG and was appointed to the Privy Council in 1939.

Walter Runciman is a Viscount (created 1937) and has been a Privy Councillor since 1908.

Henry David Reginald Margesson was created a Viscount in 1942 and has been a Privy Councillor since 1933.

Horace Wilson is a GCB and a GCMG.

Montagu Norman has been a Privy Councillor since 1923.

Let us ask ourselves seriously: are these men whom we wish to see holding the highest judicial offices in the land sitting in the Upper House and in inner councils of His Majesty?

And for good measure she included:

(a) Our city financiers who, from short-sighted (if not dishonest) motives of immediate profit, connived at Germany's financial ramp and currency manipulations over reparations and provided her with endless credit which they knew – or should have known – was being used for her re-armament.

(b) Our business men who, for their own personal profit, supplied scrap iron, etc., etc., to Germany up to the last moment.

Question 3 **'Should the persons responsible be brought to trial bearing in mind that the procedure of trial by impeachment no longer obtains?'**

The word impeachment immediately brings to mind the scene in Whitehall in 1649, when King Charles the First of England was arraigned before the High Court of Justice – a body comprising members of the Lords and Commons and some Aldermen of London – and charged with high treason. Accused of making war against Parliament, he was found guilty and executed – which today might sound illogical. Parliament is surely carrying out the government of the State on behalf of the Sovereign. So an act of treason against Parliament is an act of treason again the Sovereign as well. '*L'etat, c'est moi*,' as King Louis of France once said!

'If these (irresponsible) men had lived 200 or 150 years ago,' wrote General Sir Hubert Gough, 'they would all probably have been impeached and brought to trial.' Whether he actually had anyone in mind he does not say, but he goes on to advise that 'after this war a Royal Commission should be appointed to make a searching inquiry. Then the government of the day should present a Bill for the re-introduction of impeachment. The knowledge of what will be their fate will act as a deterrent to all who in future accept high office.'

Support for this came from Ben Greene, a Quaker. Born in 1901, he was educated at Wadham College, Oxford, was eventually appointed a JP and became interested in peace activities. For this he was imprisoned in Brixton Jail under Section 18B, but was released – after applying for a writ of Habeus Corpus – in January

1942. In 1943 he was Vice-Governor of the English National Association, which aimed at upholding the fundamental principles of the English Constitution and Civil Liberties. In some 4,000 words he offered reasons for the post-war re-introduction of impeachment, of which only a brief summary is possible:

If we are to accept the fact that it is an act of treachery to involve our Country in a useless war or to become involved in a war which could have been avoided and which allow our soldiers to meet the enemy unprepared, then we have to find some method whereby responsibility can be established. This is a constitutional question of the greatest magnitude. It is one of the peculiar qualities of the English constitution, which gave it its greatest quality and prestige and upon which the whole of the English conception of liberty is rested, that in England the greatest and most powerful men in the state could be, and were, brought to trial. This was impeachment in the High Court of Parliament. Impeachment, and above all the threat of it, maintained the purities and high standard of our public life. The English constitution, though legally in force, has been politically usurped by the Cabinet system and the rule of the party caucus.

The political caucus system of government has so corrupted the English constitution that the restoration of impeachment in itself will require a constitutional revolution. That revolution is bound to take place. The time has come to bring the present freedom of the Cabinet from legal control to a close. As they did in 1399, 1660 and 1688, the English people must one day restore again their own precious form of government under a happy combination of monarchy, aristocracy and democracy, each under control of the others and where impeachment is the control people will have over their rulers. Every Minister of the Crown will have before him the vision that perhaps one day he may stand, a lonely figure, in the Great Hall of Westminster, where no Official Secrets Acts can cover his ministerial activity, where no piece of collective responsibility can prevail, but only the cold circumstances of his stewardship will decide his fate.

Only one contributor was against any action being taken when the war was over. 'Only can those responsible be brought to book if 10% of the population can try to shoot the other 90%,' wrote a contributor anonymously described as the Headmaster of one of our greatest Public Schools, 'and if the authorities in the next world can be persuaded to do something about Neville Chamberlain.'

There were many, however, who believed that some sort of inquiry should be held. 'Let us probe into the matter,' said Trooper Frank Owen. 'Let statesmen, like other men, be held to account however mighty they may be – and the more so the mightier they be.'

'I am most firmly of the opinion that a judicial inquiry should be held and responsibility for guilt or criminal negligence be apportioned amongst those I have already referred to and any others involved, not merely for the sake of the future but in order that our public life may be lifted onto a higher plane,' thought Mrs E.O. Lorimer.

Lord Davies was not in favour of official impeachment: 'The delinquents can only be impeached before the bar of public opinion. Judge and jury must be the electorate. When the next election takes place, let those who were responsible be arraigned at the hustings, when their fellow countrymen will be able to pronounce a verdict upon the policies and action which culminated in this catastrophe.'

Although after the First World War an American orator had demanded that the German Kaiser, Wilhelm, should be captured and boiled in oil, nothing of the sort was demanded in this country in 1945. Or was it? In 1945 the Conservative Party, which had been in office for many years, was swept away in a landslide election. Was this a subconscious and a silent verdict from millions of people, whose horizons had been widened after five years of horrifying experience? But of impeachment nothing was heard.

Question 4 **'How can a Third World War be prevented?'**

The thoughts of those writing in 1943 can today be compared with what has actually taken place from that year onwards. Since 1945 we have lived in a world quite different from that probably envisaged by those who wrote half a century ago. The advent of television, the computer and the satellite has metaphorically turned our homes into a microcosm of the entire globe; nothing can happen anywhere which cannot be seen by pressing a button – almost as soon as it takes place. The telephone, the mass use of the motor car, tourism, multinational businesses have all helped to reduce the world in size. The advent of the nuclear bomb has immeasurably reduced the likelihood of global wars. What then are the views of those who were writing half way through the Second World War?

> This time we should carefully study what we did after the last war and do dramatically the opposite – no hatred or desire for revenge. The causes of war in this present age are not political or territorial but financial and economic. Man is a fighting animal; an animal who fights for food. Give him food and he can be tamed; give him the lash, the more ferocious he becomes.
>
> (Major General J.F.C. Fuller)

H.G. Wells, in his article in the *Daily Express*, had extolled those parts of the Atlantic Charter which stressed the enjoyment of all countries of the trade and materials of the world on equal terms. In addition, he had advised that every country must relinquish absolute sovereignty as far as federal needs were concerned.

Opinions differed, but this was the theme of most of the contributors to the proposed book:

> We should announce our willingness to conclude a peace on the basis of sharing the world's economic resources.
>
> (The Duke of Bedford)

> An International Authority is essential, and such a plan involves partial surrender of sovereignty.
>
> (Lord Davies)

> A World Authority with a powerful armed International Force.
>
> (General Sir Hubert Gough)

> World peace can be achieved by a system of planning, centrally directed, which will control the elements of world trade.
>
> (Lieutenant Colonel Clive Garsia)

There must be a permanent international system which will pre-
serve peace and arrange financial and economic policies for the
benefit of all nations.

> (Professor G. M. Trevelyan,
> Master of Trinity College, Cambridge)

We have been taught that the force necessary to ensure peace cannot be improvized; that if there is to be a future League of Nations
its members must somehow be committed to act before a crisis
comes.

> (Dr Alexander Lindsay, later Lord Lindsay of Birker,
> Professor of Moral Philosophy and
> Master of Balliol College, Oxford)

Following on the forecast of H.G. Wells in 1917, the Cambridge
economist, John Maynard (later Lord) Keynes, had also warned in
1919 that the perils of the future lay not in frontiers and sovereign-
ties but in food, coal and transport. Many of R.J.K.'s contributors
in 1943 had also stressed the importance of the two clauses in the
Atlantic Charter of 1941, which referred to the full enjoyment by
all countries of the trade and raw materials of the world.

There was no spirit of hatred or revenge in 1945. The Marshall
Plan, sponsored by the USA in 1947, brought economic aid in the
form of goods and money to the stricken continent of Europe,
including Germany and Austria. The United Nations organization,
inaugurated in October 1945 and joined by 51 founder members,
has been concerned with the maintenance of peace, although, in
the absence of teeth, not always successfully. Its many agencies,
including UNESCO and UNICEF, have done much for the better
ordering of global affairs, whilst the World Bank and the
International Monetary Fund have oiled the wheels of world trade.

In 1945 the wartime Allies occupied Germany and other enemy
territories, establishing military governments (control commissions) which brought back democratic systems and, at the same
time, put these countries onto a sound economic basis. 50 years
later, these countries, including Germany and Japan, are some of
the most prosperous in the world. There was certainly no hatred or
desire for revenge, such as was exhibited in the Versailles Peace
Treaty of 1919.

20

Non-Contributors

Some extracts from the contributors to the proposed book have been included in the previous chapter. Then there were 50 men and women, distinguished and not so distinguished, who replied that they were unwilling to write anything at length, some for quite legitimate reasons: they were under contract not to write for others, or they were involved with other organizations, for whose members they could not speak. Quite a few, however, sent pamphlets about these organizations e.g. The League of Nations Union, Common Wealth, The People's Common Law Parliament and The Social Credit Party, with permission to quote if necessary.

Major General J.F.C. 'Boney' Fuller had spent his life criticizing in endless books and pamphlets − it came quite naturally to him and was expected of him. But most other people were wary of committing themselves in writing − whatever their private thoughts − by criticizing their acquaintances and members of the Government or the Establishment, especially in time of war. The prospect of Brixton Prison might well have loomed in the background; a fate from which, under Section 18B, there was no appeal.

A letter signifying a reluctance to contribute at length was answered by a long one in return; a letter cajoling and pleading the recipient to accede to his request. 'I feel that no man in a democratic country such as ours and holding a position in public life has the right to say no to any request to help in the solution of an unsolved problem of today, i.e. how to eradicate that foul thing called war and protect our future youth from the slaughterhouses of Europe and the World.' 'This is indeed a democratic country, and very busy people are still free to refuse to contribute to books they don't want to contribute to,' was the final reply of one – who might have added: 'Game, set and match to me, my friend.'

Despite all his efforts, R.J.K. had no success with the 50 unwilling participants but, during the course of prolonged correspondence, they generally gave a condensed but useful answer to parts of his original Questionnaire. The failure to obtain anything in the end from Lady Astor was a disappointment. In May 1943 she had wanted to meet him for a discussion – but by August she had backed out. Another disappointment was the failure to get anything in writing from Viscount Cecil of Chelwood, who, in 1937, had been awarded the Nobel Peace Prize. He had helped to organize the Peace Ballot, a massive demonstration of deep-rooted public feeling for peace, in an attempt to save the, by then, ineffective League of Nations. 'I have expressed my views on the subject of world settlement after the war in a pamphlet which you are at liberty to quote from,' he wrote.

An enigmatic character, Tom (later Lord) Driberg, self-confessed practising homosexual and the writer of a column in Lord Beaverbrook's *Daily Express* under the pseudonym of 'William Hickey', kept up a lively correspondence with R.J.K. A former member of the Communist Party, he had become, in 1943, the Independent MP for Maldon, Essex. In 1945 he re-stood, successfully, as the Labour candidate. 'The short, final and comprehensive answer to your question is that modern wars are caused by capitalism and can only be prevented by the abolition of that system,' was his parting shot.

Another MP (Conservative, Wood Green, Middlesex) and journalist (*Evening Standard*) was Beverley Baxter. He too declined to answer at length. His view was that 'this country could never have kept Germany down. The League of Nations supplied an imaginary safeguard behind which the people of this country refused to face reality. The League did many useful things, but it never had a chance from the beginning, because the USA had failed to join it.' With the headquarters of the post-war United Nations being situated in New York, it was hoped that this error would be rectified.

144

Lady Apsley wrote on 22 June 1943: 'It is not possible for me to enter into any agitation against the present Government. Plans are being drawn up at this very moment, but they can not yet be made public. Nor can I agree to having my name associated with people you mention, most of whom have deplorable war records themselves . . .' 'Names, please, my Lady,' noted R.J.K. at the bottom of her letter. But for someone who was Senior Commandant ATS (1938), Chairman of the Women's British Legion (1942) and a Conservative MP (1943–45), it is not surprising that her Ladyship was unwilling to get herself involved.

And so thought Lord Vansittart, member of the Diplomatic Corps. 'Any attempt to revert to the past and to fix responsibility for our failure to re-arm must lead to endless recriminations, which can serve no useful purpose except to weaken our faith in democracy. I have always tried to avoid any form of recrimination myself, though I have never failed to rub in vigorously the general lesson to be derived from the failure of all three political parties.'

On the military side, two senior Field Marshals were not to be drawn – Lord Birdwood agreed with the general contents of the proposed book, but asked to be excused on account of his advanced age and the fact that he was in the throes of moving house. Lord Milne ('Daddy' Milne to his contemporaries) had been Chief of the Imperial General Staff at the War Office from 1926–33. Having expressed an interest in Moral Rearmament, R.J.K. asked him to what extent this Movement could help to prevent civilized nations reverting to war in the future. But 'Daddy' Milne also asked to be excused. 'Until,' he thought, 'we can find some way of really civilizing the creature man, wars must continue and flourish. I can not, honestly, see any way of obtaining Moral Rearmament in a pagan world.'

Of the two Admirals of the Fleet, one of them, Sir Roger (by then Lord) Keyes, was the more helpful. This distinguished and much decorated sailor had become a Conservative MP after his retirement until his elevation to the peerage in 1943. Although he was much interested in the idea of the proposed book, he very much regretted being unable to contribute; he had so many dragons to fight, he said in a long letter. 'Ever since 1930, when the Socialists inflicted the London Naval Treaty on us, I felt that

145

war was inevitable unless we had re-armed beforehand. Ramsay McDonald and Alexander were responsible for that, and a miserably weak Board of Admiralty – Baldwin was no help – and Lord Cecil of Chelwood, with his League of Nations Union and Peace Ballot, made war a certainty.' He sent a copy of the speech he had made in the Commons in 1934 aimed at Ramsay McDonald and his National Government. In this he had urged a programme of shipbuilding to replace those capital ships which would be obsolete in two years time, and which would bring our aircraft carriers and destroyers up to the number allowed by the Treaty. This would also give work to the thousands of workmen standing idle in all our dockyards. To which Sir Stafford Cripps, in his reply, had said: 'This is not the policy of HM's Government.' The other Admiral of the Fleet, the Earl of Cork and Orrery, had expressed an interest in Moral Rearmament in 1938, but felt his views were too nebulous to be of much use.

And so the endless correspondence continued during the spring and summer of 1943, mostly with friends and acquaintances or those suggested by them. Church leaders failed to help, amongst them the Archbishop of Canterbury, Dean Inge of St Pauls Cathedral and the Bishops of Chichester and Birmingham. His Grace of Canterbury regretted that, since his transfer from York, he never contributed to a symposium, but it was probable that, like the Precentor of the Chapel Royal and Domestic Chaplain to the King, they 'endeavoured to keep out of all questions which might be politically controversial.' On the scholastic side, the Provost of Eton and the Headmasters of Marlborough and Shrewsbury sent their apologies. Apart from remembering past times and invitations to Sunday Chapel (not up R.J.K.'s street!), they hinted that they were more than busy with the boys – probably a very valid excuse! The same applied to the Headmistress of Roedean, a girl's school normally situated at Brighton but now safely evacuated to Keswick, in Cumberland, for the duration of the war.

Authors were busy writing their own books. Thus S.P.B. Mais was three behind on his contract and only wrote a letter once in three months! 'But,' he said, 'my answer to your Question 4 can be given in two words: BETTER EDUCATION.'

Well-known journalists were, by and large, bound to their

proprietors, but an exception seems to have been Douglas Reed. Working for his newspaper in Berlin and Vienna during the 1930s, he had watched the situation deteriorate to the extent that he published a book *Insanity Fair*, a best seller by all appearances. This moving narrative of his presentiments of disaster was followed by *All Our Tomorrows*, a book perhaps even better remembered today.

In February 1943, R.J.K. spoke to a crowded house in Hungerford Town Hall on 'The Cause and Prevention of Wars'. This was carried a stage further a month later when, at a similar gathering, he expressed his own opinion that, although he was not intending to embarrass present leaders, those found guilty of failing to prevent the current war should be later impeached. A 'full and interesting discussion followed' on both occasions. The preparation of his proposed book was well under way by this time. Douglas Reed, however, writing from Burgess Hill in Sussex, did not think he ought to contribute, although he was in warm sympathy with what R.J.K. had said in the Hungerford Town Hall in February. 'I do not think I should be doing anything useful because you are simply putting together a mass of conflicting opinions and suggestions which leave the reader bewildered. It is like a debate with no outcome.'

The author of *All Our Tomorrows* had hit a nail on the head, for no summary appears to have been intended; the book was just meant to make people think and, hopefully, come to some conclusion themselves. And they might, who knows, do something about it!

EPILOGUE

The compilation of *Salvation or Damnation* and its intended publication may have been a passing whim on the part of R.J.K. in 1943 – he jumped from one thing to another with great rapidity – but one facet of it must have given him great satisfaction: the repeated mention of Thomas Inskip as one of the 'guilty' politicians.

In 1927, when the National Playing Fields Association was in its third year, R.J.K. was the Honorary Organizing Secretary. Always used to having his own way, however, he had come up against the Vice Chairman, Thomas Inskip, then also Solicitor General in the Government. Anxious to bring him to heel, Inskip suggested that he should become a Paid Secretary. At a meeting in the House of Commons, rather than become the paid servant of his own brainchild, R.J.K. resigned, being granted an honorarium and Life Membership of the Association. Inskip eventually became Minister for the Co-ordination of Defence and, in 1939, as Viscount Caldecote, Lord Chief Justice of England.

He may have had a feeling of euphoria in 1943, but it was not until after the death of the man R.J.K. always described as 'HIM' in correspondence that contact was once more made with the Association – after 21 years had elapsed. At the Jubilee Dinner in 1948 and at the AGM in 1950, he was seated at the top table and introduced as the Founder of the Association. He felt, no doubt, that justice had been done at last. Nevertheless, he had been deprived of his lifelong ambition of providing adequate facilities for all classes to indulge in open-air recreation in a friendly – not professional – atmosphere.

148

R.J.K. died in 1956 in his eightieth year. He had led an eventful and interesting life, but his impetuousness and outspokenness had allowed him to go so far and no further – a fact of which he was well aware. His greatest asset, of course, was his natural ability to enter into conversation with all and sundry; he was as much at home with the 'international set' in a place like St Mortiz as he was with the one-booted urchin on the Moor at Newcastle – or the Cockneys who laughed at his carnation and spats. Getting a shrewd insight into the lives of all types of people, he was able to use the top layers of society to help the less articulate ones. As a man of extremes he was a mild socialist – he forecast and wanted the Labour Government of 1945 – yet a socialite; again, always a stickler for the correct thing being done in any situation, he himself was rarely prepared to conform.

Music, flowers, good food, the putting up of a 'good show' might well be classed as showmanship; in reality, these things were no façade but an expression of his enthusiasm, optimism and *joie de vivre*. Dejection or pessimism were no part of his nature, as the unfortunate officer discovered in 1915 when, accused of lowering the morale of the Mess, he was made to stand in front of a glass and laugh and laugh – all manner and kinds of laugh – until he had learnt what laughing was.

He will be remembered as a staunch Irish Fusilier who was always ready to help the Regiment or those in it; as a pioneer of playing fields; and as a leader who gained the affection of those under him, if not, always, of those over him. He should be remembered for his enthusiasm and lack of fear of higher authority, which enabled him to push aside opposition from the old-fashioned in order, as the Rev. Howard Marshall said at his memorial service, to make many a flickering candle burn more brightly for the welfare of the nation.

A year after his death, a memorial was unveiled to him at the Aldershot Command Stadium, in the presence of a gathering of friends, relations and a large crowd waiting to watch a football match, by Field Marshal Sir Gerald Templer, Chief of the Imperial General Staff and Colonel of the Royal Irish Fusiliers. Arriving to the tune of 'The British Grenadiers', Sir Gerald, before unveiling the plaque, said that Brigadier Reggie Kentish could be remembered in Army history and legend on account of what he did for the British soldier at a time when the nation was trying to adapt itself to more modern conditions after the long Victorian age. He loved British soldiers and devoted a large part of his life to the improvement of the conditions under which they lived. At the conclusion of the ceremony the band played 'St Patrick's Day'.

APPENDIX 1: LETTER FROM COLONEL TRENAN

A letter from Colonel Richard Trenan, MBE, MC, to Regimental Headquarters, the Royal Irish Fusiliers, in 1966. The writer joined the Army as a band boy c. 1900 and was commissioned into the Northumberland Fusiliers in 1916. A staff officer at Divisional HQ during the evacuation at Dunkirk, he ended up as Colonel i/c Administration in Northern Ireland. For 40 years he wrote for *Blackwood's Magazine* under the pseudonym of 'RT'. Living at Newry, Co. Down, he was still bathing in Carlingford Lough every day at the age of 78!

* * * * *

In an earlier letter I told you that I had been reading about Brigadier Kentish and his activities with Olympic Games and sport generally for 40 years, without connecting the name with the Kentish of the Royal Irish Fusiliers; but I had brushed against the hem of his skirts twice in an earlier age; first in 1908, when I was with our 2nd Bn lying alongside your 1st Bn in Wellington Lines, Aldershot: and next, ten years later, when I was a pupil at the Senior Officers' School at Aldershot. The school was still known as the 'Kentish' school. I graduated from it as 2nd-in-C of a Bn.

The curriculum was first-class; we did everything. We had to command a section of about six men in a tactical situation, and we commanded a tank in action. Every evening we attended a lecture given by brilliant teachers such as Fuller, and by historians and politicians and theologians and every kind of crank. Each of us

151

went back to the war after three months at this school refreshed and wiser and, I am quite sure, better qualified as leaders. For this alone I have always been grateful to Brigadier Kentish.

But still more, Kentish was the man who raised the status of the soldier, and not only the soldiers of his own regiment. It was he who influenced Smith-Dorrien to abolish the town piquets at Aldershot. I was a soldier there in 1908, and I could give you a description of the soldier's life there at that time which would make your hair curl. Since the soldier was then expected to behave like a drunken guttersnipe, he lived up to the expectation. But the abolition of the piquets robbed riotous behaviour of all its glamour, there was now no fun in fighting with the red-caps and the piquets, since these were no more. It was a simple exercise in soldier psychology.

But Kentish did more than this. He induced the men of his unit to pay into a fund, and from this every man was provided with a neat blue patrol jacket for wear in off-duty periods. We in other regiments watched this with scorn, but it was envious scorn, since men of the Royal Irish Fusiliers were now strutting about Wellington Lines as if they owned the damned place, and they had indeed become a *corps d'élite*.

His next move was to introduce passes for the wearing of plain clothes by soldiers. At that time, even a colour-sergeant had to walk out in full red regalia and pipe-clay. At first the privilege was limited to periods of furlough; next he extended it for sergeants at any time when off duty, and later to other ranks with clear conduct sheets.

It was a long time before these privileges were granted by other regiments, and in my own regiment they came but slowly and were introduced only grudgingly. I myself wore my first suit of mufti three years later; I was then a sergeant. But in these three years the soldier throughout the Army had been raised in status from the drunken lout of 1908 into being a responsible citizen, respected by the public, and all of us knew at the time that Kentish of the Royal Irish Fusiliers was the man we had to thank. The difference in the morale of the army generally was just nobody's business, and not many people even now realize how much they owe to Kentish for the high quality of the troops who went to war in 1914. In 1908, if a soldier had been found in possession of even a civilian cap it would have been used as evidence of his intention to desert; by 1914, he was beginning to be treated as a human being, and desertion was almost unknown. It took a Kentish to point out the simple psychological truth that men behave in the way that is expected of them.

RT

APPENDIX 2: TREATIES, PACTS ETC. SIGNED BETWEEN 1919 AND 1941

The Treaty of Versailles, 1919

Peace treaty between the Allies and Germany. The terms were dictated by President Wilson of the USA, Clemenceau, Prime Minister of France, Lloyd George, the British Prime Minister, and Orlando, Prime Minister of Italy. Germany was not represented.

(a)   Germany was to disarm and maintain an army of not more than 100,000 men
(b)   The Rhineland was to be permanently demilitarized and occupied by the Allies for 15 years (this only lasted until 1930)
(c)   Reparations were exacted from Germany to the tune of 132 million gold marks (reduced in later years)

The League of Nations was embodied in the Treaty, but the USA declined to join, Germany was not allowed to (she joined in 1926), and Bolshevist Russia was not invited.

The Locarno Pact, 1925

Formulated in Locarno in October 1925 and signed in London in December. This guaranteed the post-Versailles Treaty frontiers between Germany and France as well as those between Germany and Belgium. This settlement of differences appeared to herald a new era of peace (the Locarno Spirit), and Germany was admitted to the League of Nations shortly afterwards, but 10 years later left

154

it. In March 1936 she entered and militarily occupied the Rhineland. Few thought at the time that it was an act of aggression for Germany to walk into its own backyard. The Council of the League of Nations resolved, nevertheless, that she had broken both the Treaty of Versailles and the Locarno Pact. After this supine attitude war became almost certain.

The Kellogg-Briand Pact, 1928

A multinational renunciation of war as an instrument of policy, suggested by Aristide Briand of France and Frank B. Kellogg of the USA. Signed in Paris in August 1928 by the USA, France, Germany, Italy, Japan and other nations of the world, including Great Britain. With Germany now in the League of Nations, there was a feeling of euphoria and an attempt to secure worldwide disarmament under the League. The Pact was hedged, however, with so many caveats that it was rendered almost meaningless.

The Stresa Conference, 1935

Attended by France, England and Italy, who agreed to oppose further breaches of the Versailles Peace Treaty of 1919, in response to Germany's declaration of rearmament in March 1935. Six months later, in October, Italy launched an attack on Abyssinia. The League of Nations declared Italy to be an aggressor and imposed sanctions on her, except for coal and oil. The effect was minimal. The League as a peacekeeper was from then on doomed. Much encouraged, Hitler remilitarized the Rhineland in 1936.

The Atlantic Charter, 1941

A by-product rather than the objective of a conference attended by Winston Churchill and Franklin D. Roosevelt at Pacentia Bay, Newfoundland, in August 1941. The Charter was nothing more than a press release; there was no official copy signed or sealed, but it did commit the United States to some sort of international organization after the war. There were eight articles:

(1) The two countries seek no aggrandisement, territorial or otherwise

(2) They desire to see no territorial changes that do not accord with the freely expressed wishes of the people concerned

(3) They respect the rights of all people to choose the form of government under which they will live

(4) They will endeavour, with due respect to their existing obligations, to further the enjoyment by all States of access, on equal terms, to the trade and to the raw materials of the world...

(5) They desire to bring about the fullest collaboration between all nations in the economic field...

(6) After the final destruction of the Nazi tyranny, they hope to see established a peace which affords all nations the means of dwelling in safety...

(7) Such a peace should enable all men to traverse the high seas and oceans without hindrance

(8) They believe that all nations of the world... must come to the abandonment of the use of force. Since no future peace can be maintained if land, sea and air armaments continue to be employed by nations which threaten or may threaten aggression outside their frontiers, they believe, pending the establishment of a wider and permanent system of general security, that the disarmament of such nations is essential...

BIBLIOGRAPHY

Cunliffe, Marcus, *The Royal Irish Fusiliers, 1793–1950*, Oxford University Press, 1952.

Fuller, J.F.C., *The Memoirs of an Unconventional Soldier*. Ivor Nicholson & Watson, 1936.

MacDonald, Lyn, *The Somme*, Michael Joseph, 1983.

Middlebrook, Martin, *The First Day of the Somme*, Penguin Books, 1984.

Pakenham, Thomas, *The Boer War*, Weidenfeld & Nicolson, 1979.

British Olympic Association, *Official Report of the VIIIth Olympiad*, Gale & Polden, 1925.

OFFICIAL RECORDS

Centre for Military Archives, Kings College, London University: The Liddell Hart Collection, 'Montgomery-Massingberd Papers' Ref. 47.

The Public Records Office: 'The River Ancre' Ref. CAB/45/135.